New York:
Sunshine and Shadow

1. (Preceding page) Eva Tanguay as Salomé, circa 1910.   2. (Above) The elevated railroad curve in Coenties Slip, looking west from Front Street, circa 1885.

Roger Whitehouse

New York:
Sunshine and Shadow

A photographic record of the city and its people from 1850 to 1915

Harper & Row, Publishers
New York, Evanston, San Francisco, London

This book is dedicated to Helga with much affection;
to Harriet and her family, whose care and
encouragement are reflected in these pages;
and to all who have ever loved, or hated,
this extraordinary city.

3. A game of "cat stick," 1898.

4. Abraham Lincoln photographed in New York at the Cooper Union, in 1860.

NEW YORK: SUNSHINE AND SHADOW.
Copyright © 1974 by Roger Whitehouse.
All rights reserved.
Printed in the United States of America.
No part of this book may be used or reproduced
in any manner whatsoever without written permission
except in the case of brief quotations embodied
in critical articles and reviews.
For information address Harper & Row, Publishers, Inc.,
10 East 53rd Street, New York, N.Y. 10022.
Published simultaneously in Canada
by Fitzhenry & Whiteside Limited, Toronto.
First Edition.
International Standard Book Number: 0-06-014616-8
Library of Congress Catalog Card Number: 73-14300
Design, layout, illustration, and mechanicals
by Roger Whitehouse.

5. The Manhattan tower of the Brooklyn Bridge with the old Harper's building to its left, in 1876.

6. The Lake in Central Park, circa 1896.

7. A carriage in the snow during the great blizzard of 1888.

Author's Foreword   VII
Introduction   VIII

The Old City   **12**   **1**
The Waterfront   13
Commerce   22
Broadway   36
The Bowery   41
Home Life   46
Rural Manhattan   62
Brooklyn and the Boroughs   77

The Exploding City   **88**   **2**
The Huddled Masses   89
Crime   124
Reform   148
Communication   173
Transportation   176
The Bridges   214

New New York   **230**   **3**
The Waterfront   231
Commerce   245
Landmarks   281
Home Life   298
Recreation   313

Photographic Credits   X
Street Index   XII
General Index   XIV
Acknowledgments   XVI

Contents

8. Guests at the Hyde ball in 1905.

9. The bridesmaids' dinner, 1905.

Author's Foreword

Although I was familiar with the picture-postcard skyline of Manhattan before I first saw it from the deck of the *Rotterdam* upon my arrival in 1967, I was totally unprepared for the face-to-face confrontation that followed. Where was New York's equivalent of the familiar past that I was so accustomed to in London—the friendly tree-lined streets, the endless rows of unspoiled nineteenth-century houses, the worn flagstones and well-scrubbed doorsteps, all comforting reassurances of those who had passed before and prospered? Not here. It seemed at first glance as though New York had never existed before the twentieth century. The city that millions of others who had arrived from Europe before me had discovered had been altered almost beyond recognition.

Other places have undergone considerable change too, but none so ruthless as here. In old photographs of Paris or London we still recognize the structure of the city, more remarkable are the transformed fashions of clothing and vehicles in the streets. In New York we see an entirely different world. Here and there an occasional building or row of houses is identifiable but totally altered in scale by its new environment. In the nineteenth century the spire of Trinity Church towered above the city—it is difficult for us to recognize it as the little black building which today huddles between the skyscrapers of Broadway.

The idea of assembling a comprehensive photographic record of the city as it used to be and of the events which so dramatically transformed it came to me while I was researching old photographs for an urban design proposal I made for the upper East Side and Queensborough Bridge area in 1970. In the more than three years it has taken to complete this book I have had the incomparable pleasure of searching through more than twenty-five thousand old photographs in public and private collections. In the final selection I have tried to represent as many aspects of the city as possible and while I have made every effort to include the best examples of photographic quality, in some cases the importance of the subject matter of a damaged or worn print rather than its quality provided the criteria for its inclusion.

One of the great delights of these old photographs is that the cameraman, unlike the illustrator, has far less control over his medium; in every shot we see faces of the past, whether through design or by chance, staring back at us over the intervening years. These old prints invite us to make that journey in reverse and in our imagination step out from behind the camera and into the scene—to become part of the continuation of that instant snatched out of time by the camera shutter, to watch and hear that old stage continue rumbling away up Broadway as we know it must have done, or to follow that clanging fire truck around the corner and wander among the people and sights of a lost age.

Perhaps it is one of the great qualities of this city that it so uncompromisingly disregards its own history, unsentimentally uprooting people, customs, and buildings on the slightest pretext. Nevertheless it is also one of its great faults, for along with the bad it has also lost much of the good. I hope this book will in some small way encourage more of an interest in the past and present of this amazing city, for it is indifference, not malice, which results in the continual devastation of so much of the richness that is still left.

Roger Whitehouse

Roger Whitehouse, Carnegie Hall Studios, 1974.

In 1524, some Algonkian Indians, descendants of the tribes that had crossed the Bering Strait from Asia to North America thousands of years before, were witness to a remarkable event. The French caravelle *Dauphine,* captained by Giovanni da Verrazano, majestically rode into their bay, the first vessel from the Old World to share these waters with their hollow dugout canoes, thirty of which immediately set out to welcome the newcomer. Although Verrazano did not land, except to send a small boat ashore to take on fresh water from a spring on Staten Island, he must have been impressed by the beauty of this great natural double harbor. On one side the treeless expanse of Long Island, on the other the mainland and, set between the crystal clear water of the two rivers, the island of Manahatin, on whose wooded slopes and rocks the Indians made their homes in long bark huts—fishing, hunting, trapping, and here and there cultivating small plots of maize.

Many other such visitors arrived during the 1500s, with the friendly Indians losing no opportunity to trade furs, skins, and food with the newcomers, but it was not until early in the 17th century that any decided to stay. Henry Hudson, captain of the *Half Moon,* in an attempt to discover a Northeast or Northwest passage between Europe and the Orient, had been forced south away from the cold and ice of the Russian Arctic by a mutinous crew. Nearly four months later, on September 3, 1609, he entered New York Bay and spent the following month exploring the river that was to be named after him, proceeding as far north as the site of Albany trying to find an open waterway to China. It was an accident, however, which was responsible for Manhattan's first white inhabitants—Captain Adriaen Block and the crew of the Dutch ship *Tiger,* which caught fire and burned to the waterline in 1613. With help from the local Indians they built huts for the winter and rebuilt their vessel, rechristened the *Onrust* (Unrest), in which they continued their journey when spring arrived.

Nearly everyone in Europe was now well aware of the favorable news of the beautiful and fertile New World, and in 1621 the Dutch West India Company was granted a monopoly for trade with the Americas and instructed to establish colonies there. Three years later, the first shipload of settlers arrived—thirty families in all, of which only eight stayed in the area on Nutten's (Governor's) Island. It was the following year, in 1625, that the first permanent settlers arrived in four ships to join them, unloading their goods and belongings on the bare rocks and grass at the tip of Manhattan. Here, immediately south of today's Bowling Green, then at the water's edge, they constructed Fort Amsterdam in the settlement they called New Amsterdam, legalizing their position with the natives in 1626 when Peter Minuit, the first governor, bought the entire island from them for the equivalent of twenty-four dollars.

At this time, in addition to building the fort, the tiny settlement had established itself with thirty dwellings, a countinghouse, and a windmill. The surrounding area soon began to see the development of small farms and homesteads such as that of Jonas Bronck, who in 1639 settled in the area now bearing his name—the Bronx. Their isolation inevitably led to increasing skirmishes with the Indians, reaching its climax with outright warfare in 1643, "the Year of the Blood," when the terrified settlers abandoned their land holdings to seek shelter in the town. There, as further protection, they constructed a timber palisade across the island in 1653, defining the location of the now famous Wall Street.

When Peter Stuyvesant was appointed governor in 1647, the thriving settlement looked very much like a Dutch town, with small brick and stone houses each with their traditional half doors and gable ends facing onto the street. The already cosmopolitan population was soon big enough to demand an end to company rule, and on February 2, 1653, New Amsterdam became the first settlement in America to receive a charter and the right to be self-governing.

But the days of New Amsterdam were drawing to a close. In Europe, competition for world trade between Great Britain and the Netherlands was becoming bitter—so much so that Charles II sent 450 men in four warships to the new colony to claim it as his. Governor Stuyvesant got little support from the 1,500 inhabitants, who by now actually favored English rule, and the surrender ceremony was undertaken without any fuss on September 8, 1664. The first proclamation of the new governor was that thenceforth the settlement would be known as the city of New York.

The next hundred years or so were to be under English rule with the exception of a short interval in 1673-74 when it reverted to the Dutch as New Orange. Under the English the city began to consolidate, acquiring its first elective assembly in 1683 and its municipal charter in 1686. By 1700 the green spaces separating the buildings had disappeared below Wall Street, and the buildings which had replaced them were often in the red-brick and marble English style with roof balustrades or ornamental chimneys. Together with the brick and tile of the old Dutch dwellings and the legally required street lanterns placed before every seventh house, the tiny city had taken on a prosperous air.

The eighteenth century saw further development, particularly in cultural directions with the opening of a library, a theater, and newspaper offices. Political awareness in the new colony increased throughout the century, erupting decisively in 1765 over the issue of the Stamp Act, when trading was curtailed with the mother country until the act was repealed the following year. In the many taverns, coffeehouses, and markets an astonishingly wide and vocal gamut of political opinion was evident, and frequent encounters were taking place between the more revolutionary elements and the forces of King George III. On January 17, 1770, when the fourth liberty pole, the dramatic symbol of the Sons of Liberty, was hacked to pieces by the redcoats, a skirmish took place on John Street at a point known as Golden Hill, and the first blood of the American Revolution was spilt, several weeks prior to the Boston Massacre.

In quick succession the Boston Tea Party and events at Lexington and Concord led to George Washington's arrival in New York in early 1776 to strengthen its defenses, followed by the arrival from Philadelphia of the city's first copy of the Declaration of Independence, which was read in what is now City Hall Park on July 9. The British soon turned their attention to the city, and by August the bay was aswarm with a gigantic fleet which had assembled an army of 32,000 to face the 18,000 whom Washington had mustered on Manhattan, and in New Jersey and Long Island.

Hostilities commenced with the Battle of Brooklyn Heights on August 26, an American defeat that paved the way for the first landing of King George III's troops at Kips Bay on September 15. As the redcoats marched south near the East River to capture the city, the patriots retreated northward to Harlem Heights, along the path of what is now Broadway, and for the next seven years, New York was occupied by the British.

When Washington made his triumphant return on November 25, 1783, the city was in ruins. Its

"In the year of Christ 1609 was the country of which we now propose to speak first founded and discovered at the expense of the General East India Company (though directing their aims and desires elsewhere) by the ship HALF MOON whereof Henry Hudson was master and factor."

Remonstrance of New Netherland.

population had dwindled by more than half to 10,000, gardens had been torn up, and the filthy, treeless streets were lined with the empty shells of burned-out or ransacked buildings. It was a fitting gesture that the rebuilding commenced with the construction of Battery Park out of the stones of the demolished fort. By the time of the inauguration of Washington in 1789, the city was already regaining some of its former beauty, and for the next year saw a whole new social life revolving around the President, who had taken up residence at 3 Cherry Street. When the capital was changed to Philadelphia in 1790, the first census showed that New York was the largest city in the United States with a population of 33,000, a figure which would almost double by 1800.

Thanks to the political stability of the new republic, the nineteenth century saw rapid economic development —in the newly opened trade with the Orient and also with the aid of the new technology developing as a consequence of the Industrial Revolution in Europe. It is with one aspect of that new technology that this book continues the story of New York. Enthusiasm for photography was such that within one month of the introduction of Louis Daguerre's system to the public, D. W. Seager, an English resident of New York, exposed the first sensitized copper plate in the New World to a view of St. Paul's Chapel on September 16, 1839, adding a new dimension to the recording of the city's history.

The principle of photography had existed since the Middle Ages in the form of the camera obscura, an aid to drawing consisting of a tent, box, or room with a pinhole or glass lens to focus an image on the opposite surface. In the early 1800s the principle of retaining the image by means of light-sensitive chemicals was developed in France by Joseph Nicéphore Niepce, who succeeded in making the first photographs of the courtyard of his house in 1816. The results of his partnership with Daguerre led to the enormously successful daguerreotype, more than three million of which were taken in the United States alone in 1853. The example from that year on the right is one of the earliest surviving photographic views of New York City, and shows the interior of its Crystal Palace, opened two years after its English predecessor on open ground north of the city at Forty-second Street and Sixth Avenue. The other view, taken by the Frenchman Victor Prévost at the opposite extremity of the city, shows the filling in of Battery Park and was made from a wax-paper negative—a technique having the added advantage that numerous prints could be made from the same original. Wax-paper negatives were followed by wet plates, each of which had to be prepared by hand immediately before exposure, until the invention of dry plates in the 1870s introduced the system of photography which is still employed today.

In addition to the hundreds of portrait galleries which opened throughout the city, the new medium soon achieved remarkable results in the hands of such photographers as Mathew Brady, who recorded the carnage of the Civil War; Jacob A. Riis and Lewis W. Hine, who used the camera as a tool for social change; Alfred Stieglitz and Edward Steichen, who explored its artistic potential; Joseph and Percy Byron, who created a unique record of New York's elite; and Alice Austen, whose sophisticated snapshots vividly recorded many aspects of city and suburban life at the turn of the century. In their hands photography became more than just an impartial observer of the city's metamorphosis—it was part of the revolution itself, making thousands aware, without the suspicion of artistic exaggeration, of the world around them.

10. Looking north toward Trinity Church during the filling in of Battery Park in 1853.

Introduction

11. The interior of New York's Crystal Palace at Forty-second Street and Sixth Avenue in 1853.

1

The Old City

"Then there lay stretched out before us, to the right, confused heaps of buildings, with here and there a spire or steeple, looking down upon the herd below; and here and there, again, a cloud of lazy smoke; and in the foreground a forest of ships' masts, cheery with flapping sails and waving flags. Crossing from among them to the opposite shore, were steam ferry-boats laden with people, coaches, horses, waggons, baskets, boxes: crossed and recrossed by other ferry-boats: all travelling to and fro: and never idle. Stately among these relentless Insects, were two or three large ships, moving with slow majestic pace, as creatures of a prouder kind, disdainful of their puny journeys, and making for the broad sea. Beyond, were shining heights, and islands in the glancing river, and a distance scarcely less blue and bright than the sky it seemed to meet. The city's hum and buzz, the clinking of capstans, the ringing of bells, the barking of dogs, the clattering of wheels, tingled in the listening ear."

From "American Notes," by Charles Dickens, describing his visit in 1842.

When rudimentary cameras first recorded views of the city in the early 1850s it consisted almost entirely of low masonry or timber structures clustered about the tip of Manhattan, extending no farther north than the area around Thirtieth Street. Beyond, and across the East River, lay open countryside punctuated with numerous farms, hamlets, villages, and the occasional summer homes of the rich.

Above the jumbled roofs of the city rose the forest of spars and rigging of the great ships which were its principal contact with the outside world—and the gleaming spires of the churches, symbolic of the most dominant influence over a way of life still centered closely on family and home.

For many, life was elegant and easy. Well-staffed households saw to it that the daily routine progressed as smoothly as possible. Elegant coaches and carriages transported affluent passengers in silks, top hats, and jewels about their endless social rounds. Those who could not afford such luxury simply walked to their destination along tree-lined streets or boarded the brightly painted Broadway stages which rumbled over the cobblestones day and night, their iron-rimmed wheels deafening passersby. The very poor found what shelter they could in hovels near the Bowery or in shanty towns on the fringes of the city.

Life was still much as it had been in the eighteenth century. Sanitary facilities consisted of outside toilets emptied periodically by the "honey wagon," and garbage disposal was successfully handled by thousands of wild scavenger pigs. Kerosene for the oil lamps, coal for the fireplace, water in barrels at one cent a gallon, all were delivered by horse and cart. The distinctive cries of street traders brought housewives and maids to the curb in the early morning with pitchers to be filled with fresh milk or wicker baskets to be laden with bread and groceries. In the local markets marble slabs were piled high with fresh meat, poultry, and fish. On bustling Broadway the continuous line of canvas awnings deflected the intense summer sun from the fine silks and merchandise displayed in the windows below.

But times were changing, not only for the city but for the entire country. Whether attracted by the glitter of California gold or news of huge fortunes such as John Jacob Astor's acquisition of twenty million dollars, immigrants poured in from over the ocean in ever-increasing numbers. As more and more arrived the city began to burst at the seams, and its already infamous slums spread uncontrollably. In response to problems such as these the Commissioner's Plan of 1811 had already established the gridiron which was enabling development to proceed on an orderly basis. But this was just a first step; a new world was evolving which would dramatically alter every facet of life as it was then known.

The photographs in this first section, taken mostly in the 1850s, 1860s, and 1870s, show old New York in its last days before the gathering storm of social and technological change broke and swept it away forever. They were chosen for their subject matter rather than by date, for much of the old city survived alongside the new—for a few years at least.

12. Looking southwest across the harbor and tip of Manhattan in 1876 from the Brooklyn tower of the Brooklyn Bridge while still under construction. This remarkable panoramic view by J. H. Beals gives us a comprehensive impression of the old city. Nevertheless, the Manhattan tower of the bridge, and the new Post Office and Western Union Building immediately to its left, herald the end of an era. Had this photograph been taken even two years earlier, the spires of Trinity Church and St. Paul's Chapel would have been the only structures other than a couple of shot towers (see plate 235) to rise above the roofs of the city.

14

The Waterfront

To begin at the beginning we must look to the sea, for this is where the Europeans who settled in New York came from, followed by the strange and exotic cargoes upon which the city built its fortune. In Dutch times the first shallow ships to come here docked at the very tip of the island at what is now the location of the South Ferry. After the Revolution, when larger craft began to appear making deeper moorings necessary, the city responded by moving out toward the sea, filling in the shallows and creating in turn, Water Street, Front Street, and finally South Street.

13. Looking north along South Street from Coenties Slip, circa 1884. The bowsprits of the great ships stretch across the muddy bustling street toward the shipping offices, storehouses and chandleries opposite. Everything needed on board was available here— canvas, cordage, blocks, oils, paints, lanterns, compasses, bells, swords, and guns. The streets beyond catered to the seagoer's other wants, and next morning like as not he would find himself lying in the gutter with an aching head and empty pockets.

14. Looking south from Peck Slip in 1876. The oyster merchants while away their time in conversation waiting for the fishing boats to return with their catch. High above their horses and carts a seaman works on the rigging of a bowsprit spanning across toward the Fulton Market on the right. On the left is the Fulton Ferry Building, from which the incessant ferryboats plied their way across the river to Brooklyn and back.

15

16

18

15. A floating grain elevator in the harbor near Fulton Street, circa 1870. These strange structures were a common sight in the waters around the city in the days of sail. Grain is being lifted out of the barge *Simcoe* by scoops on a conveyor belt in the device projecting from the right of the elevator. It was then poured into the receiving ship through hinged tubes, two of which can be seen on the nearest face of the structure, before being bagged for shipment.

16. An American full-rigged ship lying at Pier 19 at the foot of Maiden Lane, circa 1900.

17. A Down-easter lying at the foot of Fletcher Street, circa 1900. Both these views, taken by Thomas W. Kennedy, show that the waterfront had not changed much in appearance in the first fifty years that photography had recorded it. The vessels themselves, however, had undergone a subtle transformation from the 100-man clippers which had reduced the journey to San Francisco from 300 to 100 days. Now the bigger and slower four- and five-masted schooners with crews of no more than ten concentrated on the less romantic coastal cargoes of lumber and coal.

18. The Wall Street Ferry Terminal on South Street, circa 1890. When New York was still isolated as an island there were dozens of ferries connecting it to the mainland and Long Island. The Wall Street Ferry ran to Montague Street in Brooklyn and stood at the foot of Coffee House Slip, as this end of Wall Street was known. The name referred to the old Tontine Coffee House at Water Street, which in 1792 had housed the Stock Exchange.

19. Looking along Atlantic Street, Brooklyn, across the harbor, circa 1865. In the days of sail the harbor was always a panorama of billowing canvas or bare rigging as fishing boats and giant clippers went about their business or lay at anchor. In the foreground, at the foot of Atlantic Street with its line of awnings and frames spanning the entire sidewalk, are the bridge and funnel of one of the steamboats which connected the two cities from South Ferry. The brick smokestacks on the right mark the location of the Brooklyn Flint Glass Works at the foot of State Street; beyond them the trees of Battery Park are just visible.

20. The Atlantic Docks, Brooklyn, looking north from Clinton Wharf in 1878. The increasing congestion of shipping on South Street, which could offer no further room for expansion, led to the formation of a company in 1840 to convert some of Brooklyn's desolate swampland into this enormous docking and warehousing area, which by 1850 was already handling large volumes of cargo.

21. The U.S.S. "Ohio" moored in the Brooklyn Navy Yard, circa 1865. Brooklyn had previously provided yet another nautical service to the city when Wallabout Bay became a natural home for the Navy Yard in 1801. In this photograph by Mathew Brady, famous for his remarkable records of the Civil War, we see the first ship ever built there. She was completed in 1821 after four years' work and remained in service until 1883. With a length of 208 feet and a beam of 53, she was armed at various times with between 86 and 102 guns, the heaviest of which was a 42-pounder. All that remains of her now is the Hercules figurehead, which has found a resting place in Stony Brook, Long Island.

19

21

". . . the crowd on the Battery shore give three hearty cheers. The ensign is dipped and the graceful clipper with a smother of foam at her fire peak is away for the Golden Gate and the perils of Cape Horn. Once clear of the Bay and hull down on the horizon the voyage was fairly begun. A more beautiful sight can hardly be imagined than the dawn breaking with possibly two or three of these magnificent vessels in sight of each other. . . ."

From "Valentine's Manual," Volume 3.

20

Commerce

It was on the tip of Manhattan that the first trading was done with the Indians for furs, skins, and food. Ever since, and in ever more magnificent surroundings, that same site has seen the early business establishments flourish into the multimillion-dollar corporations of today whose giant skyscraper headquarters now dwarf the seventeenth-century street pattern.

22. The Erie Railway Company's office on the north corner of Coenties Slip and South Street, circa 1880. As the location of the Erie Building demonstrates, the commercial center first developed in close proximity to the waterfront—particularly necessary at a time when communication was either by direct conversation or a written message delivered by hand.

23. Battery Place at the foot of Broadway looking south, circa 1897. This was originally the site of Government House, as it had been intended that the city would also be the political and diplomatic capital. It was never occupied by the first President and Congress, however, because Philadelphia became the nation's capital almost immediately. In 1815 the building was demolished and this elegant row of six brick houses was constructed, becoming in time the ticket offices of the major steamship companies. As a result the block became universally known as Steamship Row until it was torn down to provide room for Cass Gilbert's Customs House, which was completed in 1907. The street vendor, offering lemonade at one, two, three, and five cents a glass, is standing in the intersection of the cable-car loop which turned around Bowling Green and an extension on the right which ran down to the South Ferry.

24

24. Looking west on Wall Street toward Trinity Church, circa 1872. It is difficult to think of this view as that of the world's best known commercial center, although most of the old residential buildings in the street were already occupied as offices by bankers, brokers, and insurance companies. The third Trinity Church on this site, completed in 1846, proudly towers above the street as it continued to do for the first fifty years of its existence. The Greek Revival Subtreasury Building, on the right at Broad Street, was built in 1862 on the site where Washington took his oath of office as President in 1789.

25. Looking north along Nassau Street, from the corner of Wall Street, to the post office in the old Middle Dutch Church between Cedar and Liberty Streets, circa 1860. This extraordinary building in the heart of the business section, whose steeple and interior woodwork were brought from Holland during the Revolutionary War, was originally constructed in 1730. The church suffered considerably at the hands of the British, being used as a riding school, a prison, and a hospital before being reconsecrated for public worship in 1790. It was used as a post office, a rather strange sight in the midst of a graveyard, from 1844 to 1875, at which time its massive successor was opened in City Hall Park (see plates 193 and 282).

26. Looking northwest at the corner of Pearl and Chatham (now Park Row) Streets, circa 1860. These storehouses stood at the corner where the horsecar tracks in the foreground turned north (to the right) up Chatham Street and on to the Bowery.

27, 28. Looking north up Sixth Avenue from Eighth Street in 1866 and 1876. Founded in 1832, Jefferson Market was one of the principal food markets in the city and a center of Greenwich Village life. Court was held in the assembly rooms above the market, but the real landmark was the timber fire tower from which lookouts constantly scanned the city. The alarm was given by the tolling of a great bell, which can just be seen in the open intermediate gallery, and the mad dash to the scene of the fire by the competing fire companies was instigated, the direction being indicated by the number of strokes. The Gothic Revival courthouse, now familiar as a branch of the New York Public Library, was completed in 1876 and is seen here in the lower photograph at a time when the old assembly rooms and market were still standing.

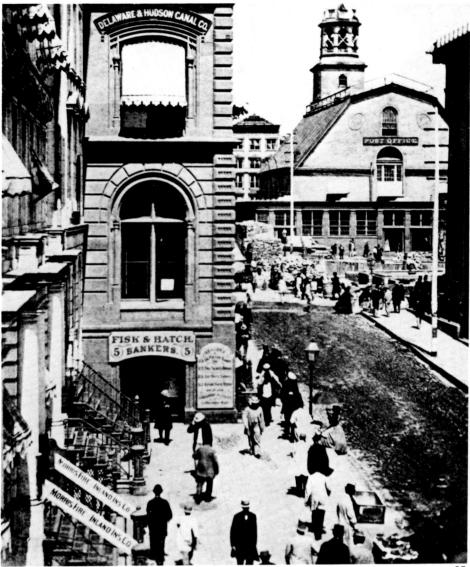

25

26

"Especially was I glad of Cup o' Tea's coop [one of the stalls in the market] and company if the great fire bell above our head began to boom. For some years after the fire engines were drawn by horses, instead of, as in the early sixties, by the volunteers running afoot, this bell was sounded from the watchtower and it was by counting the strokes that we might locate the fire. The key to these numbers was in the form of a small book with a dull pink cover. This book cost six cents and could be bought, among other places, at Taffy John's Candy Shop near the brewery at the Greenwich Avenue corner of Eleventh Street. I always kept this little book in my apron or coat pocket, for going to fires was one of my greatest desires."

From "My New York," by Mabel Osgood Wright.

27

28

29. Numbers 1-5 Hudson Street, between Chambers and Reade, looking west in 1865. The extravagance of these signs is probably the result of some shrewd salesmanship on the part of Leonard Ring, signpainter at No. 5. The elegance of this Victorian display is evident even though we cannot see the rainbow of colors in which it was undoubtedly executed. Small businesses such as this were a common sight along Hudson Street from its beginning here to its termination at Abingdon Square in Greenwich Village.

30. Looking north up Hudson Street, across Duane Street, in 1863, from the same viewpoint at the intersection of West Broadway (foreground) and Chambers Street, possibly from the roof of the Hudson River Railroad passenger station, which was built here in 1851. The trains were carried by a "dumb engine" up to Canal Street and then along West Street to the terminal at Thirty-fourth Street, where they picked up steam locomotives. On the left can be seen the "Painting" sign projecting from No. 5 Hudson Street, seen on the extreme right of the photograph on the left.

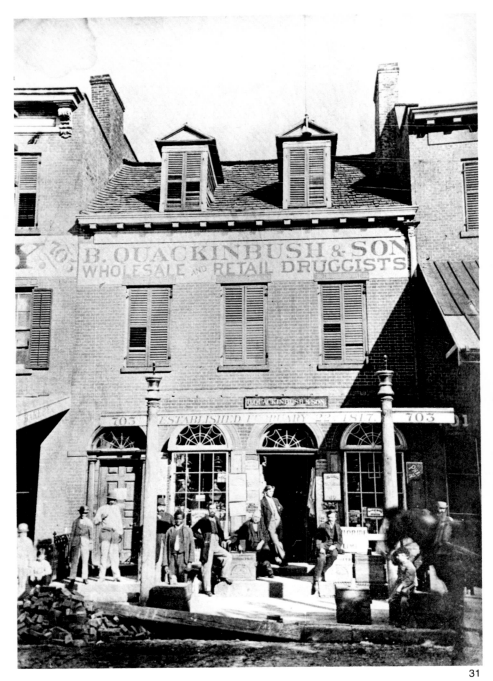

31

32

33

"As for the hoopskirt, dainty people who considered safety slipped the two lower hoops into a double facing with an embroidered or corded edge. This facing not only kept the wearer from stepping through the hoops but kept the hoops from the street mud, for street cleaning in New York was negligible in the sixties. Thus people had at least two hoopskirts and many facings, one to wear and another waiting. With four hoop-wearers in our house, the square closet in the third story resembled a small hangar of dirigibles."

From "My New York," by Mabel Osgood Wright.

34

31. B. Quackinbush and Son, wholesale and retail druggists, 703 Greenwich Street, near Amos (West Tenth) Street in 1880. This small businessman typically lost no opportunity to employ signpainters to make himself known. Even the awning posts are each surmounted by a gold mortar and pestle, which would still announce the nature of his profession even when the canvas was rolled out to shade the sidewalk, obscuring the signs above. It is probable that all the wooden fittings here were made by the inmates of the State Prison, nearby on Washington Street, who were kept busy with such tasks.

32-35. Albert Marsh's Harlem Drugstore, 1432-34 Third Avenue at 125th Street in 1865. Taken from a set of old stereopticon cards, these charming views vividly express the social importance of the corner drugstore, a uniquely American institution, in its early days. While birds sang overhead in gilded cages, hoopskirted women went about their daily marketing, while the menfolk, neatly groomed in well-brushed silk hats and broad-striped trousers, played cards or read the daily papers. This was an important location, even in the 1860s, because the old Harlem Bridge, two blocks north, was one of only five small bridges leading to the mainland. Still a small, isolated village separated from New York by miles of open countryside, Harlem first became a popular place for the well-to-do to live after the opening of the Harlem Railroad in 1837. A fleet of smart sidewheelers also regularly connected with Pike Slip via the East River, although it was not until the elevated railroad reached it in 1879 that the brownstone era began and an upper-middle-class white neighborhood developed.

Before anyone from the Old World had set foot in the New, the Indian had established a trail across "Manahatin" responding to the natural features of the land. After colonization its course endured in the bustling (and broadest) main thoroughfare of the tiny settlement. Although some discipline has since been exerted on its original meanderings, it still boldly defies the gridiron as it strikes diagonally across the island. It is reassuring to see the contortions of twentieth-century skyscrapers as they are forced, at considerable cost, to conform to the red man's response to nature centuries ago—some small recompense, perhaps, to add to the twenty-four dollars they received for the island.

36. Bowling Green in 1871, looking north from an upper window in Steamship Row (see plate 23). In 1732 the British laid out and enclosed this little oval park at the foot of Broadway to serve as a bowling green, eventually embellished by a leaden statue of King George III. Later, the popularity of both bowling and the British declined and the green was replaced by a pond and fountain. The statue, of course, was turned into musket balls for use against its regal subject. It was not uncommon to find deer, geese, and other edible wild creatures being fattened in this suitable enclosure by the local residents. It is today the oldest park in the city.

37. Looking south down Park Row toward St. Paul's Chapel, circa 1860. On the right, within the railings that then enclosed City Hall Park, can be seen the portico of the old Hall of Records. On the left, in what was known as Printing-House Square, is the New York Times Building, completed in 1858.

38. Broadway and City Hall Park, looking north from the intersection of Park Row, circa 1859. Hundreds of Broadway stages, owned by several different companies, packed the street from one end to the other creating a continuous traffic jam during rush hours. At other times of the day the situation was hardly better, for the competing drivers were often involved in hair-raising races to get to the waiting passengers ahead of their rivals. On the right is a "Harlem & Yorkville Direct" horse-drawn streetcar. From here they ran up Park Row, Chatham Street, and the Bowery to Fourteenth Street, where they picked up steam engines to continue their journey north.

39. Looking south down Broadway from the Post Office at the tip of City Hall Park, circa 1880. Representative of the changing order, the spire of Trinity Church is challenged by the tower of the Western Union Building, completed in 1875 at the corner of Dey Street. Within the circular railing at the top of the tower, the outlines of a ball are just visible. After being hoisted to the top of the pole, the ball was dropped every day, promptly on the second, to signal noon.

40. Looking north up Broadway to the Loew footbridge at Fulton Street in 1866. This intersection was for many years the busiest in the city. Here the various stage lines running north and south and those connecting the ferries east and west would lock wheels, making it impossible for pedestrians to pick a safe path between the confusion of horses and the insults being exchanged by the drivers. The local tradesmen, in an attempt to improve business, petitioned the city to build the bridge. It was a disaster, providing as it did an even better grandstand for passers-by to view the confusion and listen to the obscenities of the battling drivers. After two years the same tradesmen successfully petitioned for its removal. Beyond are St. Paul's Chapel, Astor House, and the trees of City Hall Park.

36

39

37

38

Broadway

40

"The great promenade and thoroughfare, as most people know, is Broadway; a wide and bustling street which, from the Battery Gardens to its opposite termination in a country road, may be four miles long.... Was there ever such a sunny street as this Broadway! The pavement stones are polished with the tread of feet until they shine again; the red bricks of the houses might be yet in the dry, hot kiln; and the roofs of those omnibuses look as though, if water were poured on them, they would hiss and smoke, and smell like half-quenched fires. No stint of omnibuses here! half-a-dozen have gone by within as many minutes. Plenty of hackney cabs and coaches too; gigs, phaetons, large-wheeled tilburies, and private carriages.... Heaven save the ladies, how they dress! We have seen more colours in these ten minutes, than we should have seen elsewhere, in as many days. What various parasols! what rainbow silks and satins! what pinking of thin stockings, and pinching of thin shoes, and fluttering of ribbons and silk tassels, and display of rich cloaks with gaudy hoods and linings!"

From "American Notes," by Charles Dickens, describing his visit in 1842.

41

42

The Bowery

43

The Dutch West India Company, in order to attract settlers from Holland, offered each a "bouwerij"—a strip of cleared land equipped with a house, a barn, four horses, four cows, some sheep and pigs, and some farming implements. They were mostly situated in the area between Wall Street and what is now Union Square. The thoroughfare which connected them to the city, known as Bouwerie Lane by the English, eventually assumed a notoriety and importance second only to Broadway. While the latter was the epitome of fashion and respectability, it was at night that the Bowery achieved its distinction. Its "free and easies" and "low theatres" competed with German Wein und Bier halls for those in search of merriment. Needless to say, the respectable and well-to-do were often seen here slumming or feeding their insatiable appetite for moral indignation.

41. Looking north up the Bowery from Chatham Square, circa 1858. The awnings of the stores and the row of cabs in the center of the street are typical of the city in the 1850s.

42, 43. Looking south down the Bowery from Eighth Street, showing the Seventh Regiment assembled prior to its departure for the Civil War in 1861. The old Twenty-seventh, renamed the Seventh, was the most renowned of New York's regiments. It moved into its new armory, above Tomkins Market, just out of sight to the left of the upper photograph, in 1857 and remained there until 1880.

44. The Five Points looking west on Worth Street at the intersection of Orange, Cross, and Little Water Streets, circa 1860. Immediately to the west of the Bowery at Chatham Square, the Five Points was originally the site of the collect pond in colonial days. In 1820 the respectable inhabitants finally abandoned these small clapboard houses to New York's underworld, and this intersection of five streets became the notorious focal point of degradation and crime. It was here that the city's most infamous slum, the Old Brewery, was located. One great room alone, known as the den of thieves, housed more than seventy-five people, many of whom reportedly never left its walls or saw the sunlight.

45. A New York scavenger pig, circa 1890. This pig, photographed by Jacob Riis, is representative of a major historical phenomenon. In 1819 it was officially estimated that there were twenty thousand hogs running at large in the streets of the city. At first they were a welcome solution to the problem of garbage disposal (and a cheap source of ham and bacon), but their continued existence led to New York's streets becoming the filthiest in the United States. In the 1850s, a huge sow ranged through the territory east of Chatham Square with a card tied to her tail: "I'm Paddy Doyle's Pig, whose pig are you?"

45

"Take care of the pigs. Two portly sows are trotting up behind this carriage, and a select party of half-a-dozen gentlemen hogs have just turned the corner.... Ugly brutes they are; having, for the most part, scanty brown backs, like the lids of old horsehair trunks: spotted with unwholesome black blotches.... At this hour, just as evening is closing in, you will see them roaming towards bed by scores, eating their way to the last."

From "American Notes," by Charles Dickens, describing his visit in 1842.

Home Life

49

47

Here we look at the homes of New Yorkers as they were in the mid-nineteenth century in the days before the main brownstone expansion. These are memories of an age when the family gathered around the piano in the front parlor to sing the latest tunes or quietly sat before the fireplace reading the eagerly awaited latest novel of a favorite author—a time when the written word or an evening out at a lecture or at the theater was a treasured means of contact with new ideas and the outside world.

46. Chambers Street at Centre Street, looking northeast along City Hall Place to St. Andrew's Church at Duane Street, circa 1860. The same view today would be looking through the arch of the Municipal Building. Although business interests are already represented by Bruce's New York Type Foundry, this charming photograph is very typical of the city of a century past, almost European but with its own special chaos of widely diversified building heights. Shown here to excellent advantage are the slightly raised granite slab crossings, which were masterpieces of urban design: they clearly indicated the place where pedestrians could cross, were slightly raised so rain water would immediately drain off, provided a more suitable surface for walking than did the treacherous cobblestones, and of necessity caused the traffic to slow down.

47. Looking north up State Street to the foot of Broadway, circa 1875. The buildings on the left are the beginnings of Broadway facing onto Bowling Green, and on the right the back of Battery Place, later to become Steamship Row (see plate 23). At this time the road surface was loose gravel and the area entirely residential, a staggering contrast with the same area today.

48. Looking south down Sixth Avenue from Eighth Street toward St. Joseph's Church in 1866. Greenwich Village is one of the oldest residential areas of the city to survive as such, a result of its original isolation so far out in the country north of the commercial center. First the site of palatial summer homes, it developed rapidly in the early nineteenth century as a haven for the population of New York City attempting to escape the annual scourge of yellow fever. It was not absorbed by the expanding city until 1830.

49. Numbers 60 and 62 Oliver Street, at Oak Street, looking east, 1899. The clapboard house on the corner was the residence of George Washington. The three-story building next door belonged to DeWitt Clinton, mayor and then governor of New York, and displays his coat of arms beneath the center upstairs window.

48

50

51

"GEORGE WASHINGTON, with his right arm upraised, sits his iron horse at the lower corner of Union Square, forever signalling the Broadway cars to stop as they round the curve into Fourteenth Street. But the cars buzz on, heedless, as they do at the beck of a private citizen, and the great General must feel, unless his nerves are iron, that rapid transit gloria mundi."

From O. Henry's "The Voice of the City."

50. Lafayette Place (now Lafayette Street), looking north from Great Jones Street in 1866.

51. LaGrange Terrace, otherwise known as Colonnade Row, on Lafayette Place, circa 1890.
In 1826, Lafayette Place was cut through the center of the old Vauxhall Gardens, the half adjacent to the Bowery being retained as a public park. On the other half, in 1830, Seth Geer erected these nine residences with twenty-eight marble columns and a pediment cut by the prisoners at Sing Sing. Initially it was considered amusing that such palatial splendor should be built so far from the city, for in those days the terrace stood alone. Such criticism was short-lived, however, for as development moved north this soon became New York's most fashionable address. The demolition of more than half the terrace in 1901 was a disaster; although the four remaining units are designated landmarks, the overall unity has been considerably weakened.

52. Looking north up Fourth Avenue (now Park Avenue South) from Union Square at Fourteenth Street, circa 1860. The city council laid out Union Square as an oval park with paths and a fountain in 1845, at which time some of the residences seen in this photograph had already been built. On the northern edge of the city at that time, it was an extension of the aristocratic quarter which centered on Lafayette Place and Bond Street. The statue of George Washington has since been relocated inside the park.

*"Fifth Avenue is very muddy
above Eighteenth Street, and
there are no blocks of houses
as there are downtown, but
only two or three on a block.
Last Saturday we had a picnic
on the grounds of Mr.
Waddell's country seat way up
Fifth Avenue (37th Street) and
it was so muddy I spoiled my
new light cloth gaiter boots."*

*From "The Diary of a Little
Girl in Old New York,"
written by ten-year-old
Catherine Elizabeth Havens,
in 1849.*

53

54

55

53. Looking east along Twenty-ninth Street from Broadway in 1869. As the residential streets extended farther north, the last remnants of the rural life were engulfed. The Caspar Samlar farmhouse, otherwise known as the Anderson Cottage, was the last of the old farmhouses which had once stood on lower Broadway and is seen here in the year of its demolition.

54. Looking south down Fifth Avenue from Twenty-first Street, circa 1865. As Broadway became increasingly commercial, the well-to-do began to consider Fifth Avenue the most fashionable address. It was originally proposed in the gridiron plan of 1811, but it was not until 1824, when the population rose above 100,000, that it first began to develop on the few blocks between Waverly Place and Ninth Street. At the time of this photograph the avenue was still being laid out between Forty-second and Fifty-ninth Streets, although there were few buildings to be seen that far north. On the right is the Union Club, the most aristocratic sanctuary for men in New York, and facing it on the southwest corner of Twenty-first Street the Dutch Reformed Church.

55. Looking west along Twenty-first Street from Broadway in 1865 toward the same intersection seen in the previous photograph. This view reinforces the character of what was then the main residential section of the city.

56. Looking west along Fifty-fourth Street across Fifth Avenue, circa 1865. The farther uptown one traveled, the barer the landscape became. St. Luke's Hospital, on the right, was the leading Protestant Episcopal hospital in the city when it was founded here in 1854. It stood alone except for the stable opposite at 4 West Fifty-fourth Street, now owned by John D. Rockefeller, III.

57

58

59

61

57, 58. The front parlor of 136 Joralemon Street, Brooklyn, in 1865. This charming pair of photographs shows the interior of the house of a well-to-do family. All the details are typical: the chandeliers, the ponderously framed paintings, and the ornate design of the moldings, wallpaper, carpet, and furniture. The family sitting together reading and the young woman playing the piano are representative of a whole way of life revolving around the family, who had to entertain themselves and each other in an era which offered few alternatives.

59, 60. Alice Austen and friends on the veranda, Staten Island, circa 1890. These first two photographs of the many by her in this book are the work of Alice Austen, seated on the left in the above photograph, who has left us a remarkable legacy of scenes of her youth on Staten Island and in New York across the harbor. The "good old days" that these two photographs conjure up were the prerogative of only the tiny minority that could afford them. It is a tragic footnote that over the years the Austen family's wealth eroded away and in her later life she spent all but her last year in the Staten Island poorhouse.

61. Summer house of Mr. and Mrs. George Satterlee, Grimes Hill, Stapleton, Staten Island, in 1863. Looking back at this tea-party group, over what is little more than a hundred years, it is awesome to contemplate the staggering gulf which exists between our age and theirs, with its strict observance of codes of class, morals, and manners.

Rural Manhattan

Since 1800 the northern limits of the city had mushroomed from the vicinity of Canal Street, threatening the Madison Square area on Fifth Avenue by the middle of the century. Farther west it was even reaching into the thirties. Up to Fourteenth Street the development was fairly complete; above that, new row houses were intermingled with open lots, farms, building sites, and shanties. At Fortieth to Forty-second Streets the Croton distributing reservoir still stood on open ground, although the streets had been laid out around it in accordance with the 1811 gridiron plan. Beyond, open countryside, farms, and small settlements were interspersed with the summer houses of the rich overlooking the Hudson and the East River.

63

62

64

62. Looking west along Seventy-first Street, across Madison Avenue, toward Central Park in 1885. Standing alone, on the west side of the park, is the original Seventy-seventh Street building of the American Museum of Natural History, completed in 1877.

63. Looking north across Fourth (now Park) Avenue at 100th Street in 1875. Here the old New York & Harlem Railroad trestle spans the low ground between 100th and 110th Street, before it was replaced by the existing masonry structure. The natural topography of the city is clearly visible, dotted only by odd farms and isolated rows of brownstones. Mount Morris Park, still covered with its original foliage, stands out prominently, at 120th Street.

64. Looking south down Fourth (now Park) Avenue from Fifty-third Street in 1860. This remarkable photograph shows the Harlem Railroad tracks as they originally were, on the street surface, running directly down to the terminal point, which was then at City Hall Park. On the left is the Steinway piano factory between Fifty-first and Fiftieth Streets.

65. Looking south down Park Avenue from Ninety-fourth Street, circa 1885. In this later photograph the original trench, over which each street was spanned with a bridge, has been recently covered in. The only evidence now of the railroad running below are the frequent ventilation shafts and the entrance to the station at Eighty-fourth Street.

65

66. Looking west along 116th Street at Madison Avenue, circa 1895.

67. "Carnegie Hill"—shanties near Fifth Avenue at Ninety-first Street, circa 1895. As the city extended farther and farther north it pushed before it the ever-present crop of shanties and goats. Their presence here was not accidental; in many instances they were the homes of the poverty-stricken immigrant day laborers who were laying out the roads, blasting through the rock, and helping construct the mushrooming rows of brownstones.

68. Skating in Central Park, looking southwest toward Fifty-ninth Street and Sixth Avenue in 1859. Taken during the construction of the park, this photograph shows a group of shanties and cottages approximately in the area of Fifty-ninth Street (now Central Park South) and Sixth Avenue. Although by this time the streets had been laid out and graded, they were not yet surfaced, and these early buildings did not relate to them geometrically.

66

67

68

69. The Sheep Meadow in Central Park, circa 1880. The location of the 800-acre park grew out of a dispute in 1850 when the legislature was entertaining the idea of purchasing Jones Wood on the East River as a public area. After becoming a political issue in the 1850 mayoral campaign, the present inland site was chosen as being unsuitable for anything else. In 1857 the shanties, swill mills, glue factories, and other structures were torn down, the squatters and hogs were evicted, and the park began to take shape, finally being completed in 1876 after delays caused by the Civil War.

70. Looking east toward Fifty-ninth Street and Central Park across Sixth Avenue in 1859. Professor T.S.C. Lowe never succeeded in crossing the Atlantic in his balloon "The City of New York," for which purpose it had been designed, but he made many ascents from Central Park and elsewhere.

71. Bloomingdale Lane in 1862. Bloomingdale Village was situated to the west of the park near what is now Broadway and Sixty-eighth Street. The old Bloomingdale Road, which traversed Manhattan diagonally, eventually became part of Broadway.

72. Looking south down the East River from the foot of East Fifty-third Street in 1859. On the eastern edge of Manhattan, small landings like this were a common sight and were much used by the river-front industries and farms of Turtle Bay, as this area was then called.

73. The "Undercrust" shanty on Fifth Avenue, circa 1870. Situated just above Fifty-ninth Street, this precursor of the soda fountain probably did an excellent trade with thirsty families out for a day in the park.

74. Looking west on Eighth Avenue at Eighty-fourth Street, circa 1870. The Central Park House probably catered to those out for a jaunt in their carriages as well as to neighborhood residents. One wonders if the centrally placed line of buttons on the early police uniforms were put there intentionally to accentuate the corpulence of the occupant, made all but inevitable by having an inn on his beat. Police were banished to "the Goats," as the desolate uptown shanty areas were called, as a form of punishment—possibly for arresting a felon with too much influence in high places.

70

71

72

73

74

75. Hamilton Grange, circa 1880. The Grange, built in 1802 as the country seat of Alexander Hamilton, has been in storage for the last seventy years on a site adjacent to St. Luke's Hospital. Here it is seen in its original location at what is now the intersection of 144th Street and Amsterdam Avenue. Within the enclosure in the foreground are the thirteen trees representing the original states of the Union.

76. The Dyckman House at Broadway and 208th Street, circa 1900. Another early dwelling of a very different character, the Dyckman House, shows a strong Dutch influence and is the only remaining eighteenth-century farmhouse in Manhattan. The interior contains the original family furnishings and is well worth visiting.

When "Breuckelen" was established as a town in 1667 it consisted of a few wooden shacks facing its neighbor across the river. Robert Fulton's invention of the steam ferry (Fulton Streets in Manhattan and Brooklyn were renamed after him when the first ferry connected them in 1814) actually made Brooklyn Heights more accessible to the Wall Street area than most of Manhattan, resulting in its rapid "colonization" in the nineteenth century. By 1834 it had grown enough to become a city in its own right, with a population of more than 30,000. It was not until 1898, after the bridge had mixed the lifeblood of the two great cities together so inextricably they had become one, that they were consolidated into Greater New York City together with the other boroughs. In the early nineteenth century the Brooklyn hinterland, Queens County, and the Bronx consisted of open farmland scattered with numerous villages and hamlets. Across the harbor, "Staaten Eylandt" was first referred to as such by Henry Hudson in 1609, only to be renamed after the Duke of Richmond when the English captured New York in 1664.

77. Fulton and Court Streets, Brooklyn, looking south from Pierrepont Street toward the Court House, circa 1865. Brooklyn City Hall (now Borough Hall) on the right was completed in 1851.

78. DeKalb Avenue and Fulton Street, Brooklyn, circa 1860. Much of the rigid posing in early photographs was due to the inability of the long exposures needed to capture movement. As a consequence the photographer had to instruct everyone to stand still to prevent "ghosts" such as the one in front of the delivery wagon at the right.

79. Sheepshead Bay Church, Brooklyn, in 1887.

80. T. A. Morehead's store, Flatbush, in 1886. These two photographs from a young girl's snapshot album vividly portray the essence of the more rural areas. The view from behind a horse must have been a very common one; the caption below the original print simply reads "Ma's team."

77

"*For our architectural greatness consists in the hundreds and thousands of superb private dwellings, for the comfort and luxury of the great body of middle class people—a kind of architecture unknown until comparatively late times, and nowhere known to such an extent as in Brooklyn.*"

Walt Whitman, 1861.

Brooklyn and the Boroughs

78

79

80

81. Shanties at the foot of Court Street, Brooklyn, in 1878.

82. Brooklyn shanty dwellers, circa 1880. It is evidence of Brooklyn's late development that a scene like this could exist in such a prime location less than a hundred years ago.

83. An icehouse on Staten Island, circa 1895.

84. A woman and her cow, Eighth and Flatbush Avenues, Brooklyn, circa 1885. Pointing to a much more resourceful life, these two photographs illustrate the two ways of getting fresh milk before the turn of the century, either from a cow or an icebox. The keeping of livestock was common in the city, particularly on the part of immigrants who considered such possessions a necessity of life.

81

82

84

85. Jamaica Road, Brooklyn, in 1911. The little wooden building on the right is the Pleasant Point Pump and Hose Company No. 1's firehouse. One can only assume that the large ring suspended on a wooden frame at the edge of the picture acted as a fire gong, although one is at a loss to know how the equipment was transported urgently to the scene of the fire from a location which gives every appearance of being surrounded by a swamp.

86. The Bronx River at West Farms looking north, circa 1885. The left bank of the river is now the site of the Sheridan Expressway just below the Botanic Garden.

87. Looking out over the farms toward the advancing city of Brooklyn, circa 1885.

85

87

86

''As there is only the great
bridge above, which helps the
country road across the little
stream, and the little
footbridge below, and as there
is no path or road,—all the
houses fronting the water,—the
Bronx [River] here is really
the only highway, and so
everybody must needs keep a
boat. This is why the stream is
crowded in the warm
afternoons with all sorts of
water crafts loaded with whole
families, even to the babies,
taking the air, or crossing
from bank to bank in their
daily pursuits.''

From ''A Day at Laguerre's,
and Other Days,'' by F.
Hopkinson Smith, 1892.

The Exploding City

"Those who live at a distance, and know the city only through the papers, suppose it to be as wicked as Sodom and as unsafe as Gomorrah in the time of Lot. As a home it has few attractions to a stranger. Its babel and confusion distract and almost craze. Its solitude is distressing. In the midst of a crowd the stranger is alone. He might live or die without any one's knowing or caring. The distinguished man, or well-to-do merchant from the country, has no deference paid to him. He is jostled by the crowd, trampled down by the omnibus, or run over by the market vans."

From "Sunshine and Shadow in New York," by Matthew Hale Smith, 1869.

When City Hall was completed in 1812, only the front and sides were finished in white marble—the back was constructed with simple freestone, for none of New York's 100,000 inhabitants imagined the city would ever extend north of it. By 1850 the city had already reached Thirtieth Street with a population of 700,000, and even this figure would double by the mid-1860s. By 1915, more than 5,000,000 people from all walks of life and from all corners of the earth would call themselves New Yorkers.

The city had worked well in the days when its crops and livestock were tended in the area of Madison Square and the length and breadth of it was no greater than an hour's walk. But after 1850, with the immigrants pouring in ever faster and with a natural population growth of its own, it could not cope. Slums and poverty spread like wildfire, the old techniques of sanitation, transportation, and communication were totally inadequate, and outbursts of violence and mass rioting pointed clearly to deeper problems. Little leadership or assistance could be expected from City Hall, for the political scene had regressed to one of outright corruption, the "elected" politicians using the mobs and street gangs to coerce votes in their favor in return for protection.

But necessity is the mother of invention, and in addition to the army of social reformers who were rising to put things to rights, a whole generation of what were loosely termed "engineers" and "scientists" turned their talents to solving the problems of mass urban living. Harnessing the power of steam, they developed the railroads and converted them for use in the city, often with more of an eye toward ingenuity than comfort. Electricity, the greatest single discovery of all, provided a means of transmitting that power conveniently over long distances, and the problems of lighting, heating, power, transportation, and communication were revolutionized in one bold stroke. The construction of the great bridges made the outlying boroughs accessible. Steam shovels and pile drivers and cement, cast iron and steel-beam construction, revolutionized the building industry, and the city began to reach upward as well as outward. Finally, at the turn of the century, the internal-combustion engine and the development of the automobile completed the revolution which transformed the city into a gigantic, complex metropolis.

The following photographs were chosen to illustrate some of the forces which demanded the metamorphosis, and the social and technological revolution which brought it about.

88. Looking southwest across the harbor and tip of Manhattan from the east pier of the Brooklyn Bridge in 1908. The early-twentieth-century city was a festival of new technology. On the bridge below, an unprecedented engineering feat in itself, run cable cars from the terminals in City Hall Park and Brooklyn. On the roadways the first automobiles, electric cars, and buses compete with the rapidly disappearing horse. Alongside the covered-in piers, steamboats lie together with the last remaining sailing craft and declining ferries. To the left towers the newly completed Singer Building, then the highest building in the world, made possible not only by means of new construction techniques but also by development of the elevator.

90

The Huddled Masses

As news of the good life in America spread, hesitancy to make the long and arduous journey changed to eagerness in the slums and ghettoes of Europe. First the Irish, Germans, and Scandinavians and then the Italians, Austro-Hungarians, and Russians, especially Russian and Polish Jews fleeing persecution, poured across the sea. Between 1860 and 1900 more than thirteen million immigrants arrived to begin a new life. But the gold that the streets were reputedly paved with was not always destined for the new arrivals—they had first to survive the treacherous path which led through the slums and sweatshops. For the majority, it ended in an inescapable morass of further exploitation and poverty.

89. Immigrants on the deck of the S.S. "Pennland" in 1893.

90. "The Steerage," taken by Alfred Stieglitz in 1907. It cost about thirty dollars to make the journey to New York from Western Europe, including the money which was theoretically supposed to guarantee independence upon arrival. The sum which went to the steamship company gave passengers the choice of the stench and darkness of the bare-walled hull below the waterline at the approximate level of the steering gear, hence the name "steerage," and the exposure of the deck.

89

89

93

91

94

92

91, 92. Immigrants in Battery Park outside Castle Garden, circa 1890. Originally a fort, Castle Clinton was built in 1812, the same year as City Hall, as a defense against the British. In those days, before the filling in of Battery Park (see plate 10), it was an island some 200 feet from the shore. In 1822, Congress ceded it to the city and it became the principal opera house, hosting such performers as Jenny Lind, the Swedish Nightingale. In 1855 it was converted into an immigration bureau, which purpose it served until the completion of facilities on Ellis Island in 1892. These tumbled heaps of baggage probably represent the entire worldly possessions of their owners.

93. Children's roof-garden playground at Ellis Island, circa 1900. When Castle Garden became too small to handle the influx of immigrants, they were taken by steamer to Ellis Island, where the new facilities could handle up to 5,000 newcomers a day. To celebrate their arrival these children have each been given an American flag, with which they are unfamiliar, if we can judge from the girl on the left who has decided the stripes should go up and down.

94. An inspector examining eyes on Ellis Island in 1913. Arrival in America by no means meant that the ordeal was over, for medical inspections were thorough. If this man was found to have trachoma, a large "E" (for Eyes) would be chalked on his back and he would be sent home on the next ship. Similarly, "H" indicated heart disease, "L" a limp, and, saddest of all, a simple cross in a circle, indicating "feeble-minded."

95. The quarantine side-wheeler "James W. Wadsworth," circa 1895. If contagious diseases were suspected, newcomers were sent into quarantine on Staten Island as they had been since the 1840s, despite local opposition which in 1858 resulted in a riot during which the hospital was burned down by neighbors who suspected it of being the source of the yellow-fever epidemics. These men, all wearing their best suits for the occasion, have finally been released and are eagerly looking across the harbor toward the awaiting city on the final step of their momentous journey.

96. Looking west along Delancey Street from near Essex Street in 1906. The lower East Side was synonymous with the immigrant and almost exclusively Jewish. Conditions were appalling. The Tenth Ward was the most crowded slum in the world, in whose tenements the immigrants were packed at an average of 522 per acre, nearly five times as many as in the other wards of Manhattan. Alarmed by these conditions and in response to the cholera epidemic of 1867, the city banned "dark bedrooms," unlit rooms in the center of the tenement, and in 1869 ordered 46,000 windows cut into existing dwellings. In 1879 the well-known dumbbell-shaped "old law" tenement plan was introduced as an attempt to provide some minimal ventilation. These soon became more fearsome slums as the air shafts were blocked with refuse—acting only as chimneys for the explosive fires which all too frequently occurred. When the Housing Commission met in 1900 after thirty-three years of reform, it had to admit the situation was worse than ever.

97. Stores on Clinton Street, near Delancey Street, in 1908.

98. Underneath the El on Division Street, near Pike Street, in 1910.

99. Barefoot boy on Delancey Street near Suffolk Street in 1908. Traditionally the immigrant Jew became a tailor and the lower East Side abounded in scenes such as these. Their wages and piece work rates were pitiful, with a pair of completed pants bringing perhaps fifty cents. Many deliberately went hungry and worked to a point of exhaustion to save enough money to escape such conditions.

96

97

98

99

"Between buildings that loomed like mountains we struggled with our bundles . . . through the swarming streets of the ghetto. . . . I looked about the narrow streets of squeezed in stores and houses, ragged clothes, dirty bedding oozing out of the windows, ash cans and garbage cans cluttering the sidewalks. A vague sadness pressed down my heart, the first doubt of America. . . . I looked out into the alley below, and saw pale faced children scrambling in the gutter. 'Where is America?' cried my heart. America, it turned out, was uptown."

The account of a young Jewish immigrant girl.

101

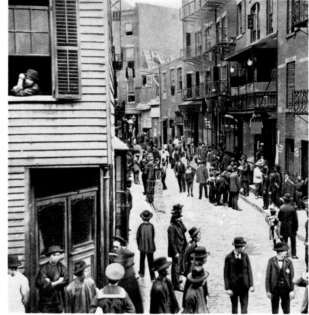

102

103

100. An egg stand in Hester Street in 1898.

101. Looking east along Hester Street from near Essex Street in 1899. This, the most famous street market in the city, was the focal point of the lower East Side ghetto. On Fridays in particular its animation became intense as thousands upon thousands of the Jewish immigrants who were crammed into the surrounding slums prepared for the coming Sabbath.

102. Chinatown on a Sunday morning, circa 1895, looking south down Doyers Street from Pell. Many other peoples made up New York's population, even if not in such great numbers as the Jews. Although this is still the most serpentine and erratic street in New York, the balconies, clapboards, and old shop fronts have disappeared in favor of modern restaurants. The Chinese population of the area rose from 1 in 1858, to 12 in 1872, to 700 in 1880, to many thousands by the turn of the century—despite the Chinese Exclusion Act of 1882, which put an official stop to immigration.

103. A vegetable stand in Mulberry Bend, circa 1895. In the Italian section the "Banca P. Caponigri" also serves as "Ufficio Postale Governativo No. 23." The man with his hands up to his face is Jacob A. Riis, author of *How the Other Half Lives* and *The Battle with the Slum* and photographer of many prints in this book. Arriving in New York from Denmark in 1870, he experienced the degradation of the immigrant from close quarters. Often jobless, hungry, and homeless, he persevered until he succeeded in becoming a police photographer for the *Tribune*. His photographic records of the plight of the helpless became an important instrument in the institution of reform measures. In this photograph he has probably been caught by his assistant while giving stage directions to the owners of the stall—for although his subjects were always real, the situations were often posed.

104. Looking south down Cherry Street, circa 1890.

105. "Paradise Alley" on the west side of Gotham Court, Nos. 36-38 Cherry Street, near Pearl Street, circa 1885. Just two blocks from the East River, Gotham Court, also known as Sweeney's Shambles, was built by a benevolent Quaker in 1851 as a direct response to the shocking living conditions of the poor. Within ten years it had deteriorated to such an extent that when the Old Brewery was demolished it gained the reputation of the most squalid slum in the city. It comprised two rows of five-story tenements under a common roof and housed more than a thousand people—principally Irish but with some blacks and Italians. Conditions were terrible; of 183 children born over a period of three years, 61 died before they were a few weeks old, some of them being killed by huge rats. The vaulted sewers from which the rodents came, running beneath the alleys at either side of the block, also served as hiding places for fugitives from the law, known as "Swamp Angels," until the police had the gratings permanently secured.

106. Allen Street, third floor front, August 4, 1916. With the El roaring past below, these children of the lower East Side demonstrate their improvised bedroom. The sweltering summers were the greatest trial for the crowded slum dwellers, and to escape the heat many slept on roofs, window sills, sidewalks, and fire escapes. The first hot nights of June brought the inevitable crop of fatalities of those who rolled off and fell to their death while sleeping.

107. The rear alley of a block of tenements in Elizabeth Street in the summer of 1903. These rear yards served as both laundries and playgrounds. Running water was unknown and had to be obtained from hydrants, several of which can be seen down the center of the photograph. At the right is the roof of a row of forty-four water closets, or "school sinks" as they were universally known, the name probably originating from the public schools in which they were first installed.

104

106

105

"One block contains 382 families. Persons composing these families were, 812 Irish, 218 Germans, 186 Italians, 189 Poles, 12 French, 9 English, 7 Portuguese, 2 Welsh, 39 Negroes, 10 Americans. Of religious faith 118 represented the Protestant, 287 were Jews, 160 Catholics; but of 614 children, only 1 in 66 attended any school. Out of 916 adults, 605 could neither read nor write. In the same block there were 33 underground lodging-houses, ten feet below the sidewalk, and 20 of the vilest grog-shops in the city. During five hours on the Sabbath, two of these grog-shops were visited by 1055 persons,—450 men and 445 women, 91 boys and 69 girls."

From "Sunshine and Shadow in New York," by Matthew Hale Smith, 1869.

"There were nine in the family: husband, wife, an aged grandmother, and six children. . . . All nine lived in two rooms, one about ten feet square that served as parlor, bedroom, and eating-room, the other a small hall-room made into a kitchen. The rent was seven dollars and a half a month, more than a week's wages for the husband and father, who was the only bread-winner in the family. That day the mother had thrown herself out of the window, and was carried up from the street dead. She was 'discouraged,' said some of the other women from the tenement."

From "How the Other Half Lives," by Jacob A. Riis, 1890.

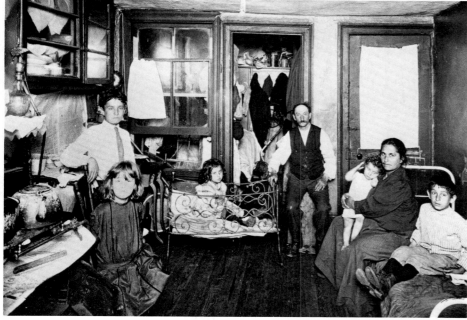

109

108, 109. New York tenement interiors, circa 1905.
Despite the obvious poverty and hardship that are
evident in each of these examples, there is a
refreshing air of cleanliness, particularly in the proud
pose of the woman with her gleaming stove, and the
children's neat clothes which testify to defiance of the
circumstances into which they have unwillingly been
trapped. It is not surprising that others did not fare so
well in the battle.

**110, 111. An East Side tenement sink and
bedroom, circa 1910.** The child is bathed and the
underwear laundered at the same time. Photographed
by Lewis W. Hine, who like Jacob Riis used the
camera as a tool to awaken an apathetic America to
the terrible realities of poverty.

110

111

112. A Ludlow Street sweatshop, circa 1890. In the late nineteenth century the law prescribed a maximum workday of ten hours, forty-five minutes for lunch, with no children under sixteen employed unless they could read and write English. But the law did not reach into the sweatshops—apartment rooms acting as homes and factories to families of tenant workers who were enslaved by their poverty and isolated by their ignorance. The incredibly small sum of money they were paid—this family received forty-five cents a dozen for finishing knee pants—was just enough to cover their rent and keep them from rebellion but not enough to allow them to escape or educate themselves. The fact that the boss was often the landlord added the threat of eviction for the imprisoned occupants.

113. Bohemian cigarmakers in their tenement, circa 1890. More than half the Bohemians (Czechs) in the city were "employed" as cigarmakers. Again the family is entombed in a tiny room in which they both work and live, making cigars from tobacco supplied by their boss. He probably paid them about four dollars a thousand, at which rate, their health and endurance permitting, they would earn about twelve dollars a week, out of which three would have to be returned for rent.

114. Sabbath eve in a Ludlow Street coal cellar, circa 1895.

113

114

115. Looking north along Clinton from Delancey Street, 1906. Part of the self-perpetuation of poverty was that it required every member of the family to work, so that children were denied the education which ultimately was their best possibility for escape. There are no fewer than fourteen newsboys at this intersection waiting to pounce on the approaching trolley as it rounds the corner or is stopped by the policeman. These "street Arabs" were refugees from broken homes and poverty all over America and were fiercely independent. Newspaper Row (by City Hall) was their headquarters, where they slept in sandboxes or huddled together over warm gratings until the Children's Aid Society or Newsboys' Homes took them in. These institutions encouraged their enterprising motives and never responded with charity. Instead, loans were granted to set them up in business with a bootblacking box or a supply of newspapers—all of which had to be paid back uncompromisingly together with a charge of six cents each for a bed or a meal. From these beginnings an astounding number rose to important positions in society, epitomizing for many the true spirit of America.

116. Bootblacks at Park Row and Broadway, 1896. This photograph by Alice Austen shows these young boys in a choice location for their trade, for it was here that the horsecars and cable cars turned round and waited outside the Post Office at the tip of City Hall Park. In the background is Astor House.

117, 118. Children gathering firewood, circa 1900. Not only did children have to assist their parents in the tenement sweatshops; they were also sent out to forage for any pickings the street might have to offer. In these photographs by Jessie Tarbox Beals we see firewood being collected which, whether obtained from a demolished building or broken packing crates, was free fuel for the stove in the freezing tenement.

115

116

'' 'We wuz six,' said an urchin of twelve or thirteen I came across in the Newsboys' Lodging-house, 'and we ain't got no father. Some on us had to go.' And so he went, to make a living by blacking boots. The going is easy enough. There is very little to hold the boy who has never known anything but a home in a tenement.''

From ''How the Other Half Lives,'' by Jacob A. Riis, 1890.

117

118

119

120

121

122

123

"Seventy-two dead babies were picked up in the streets last year. Some of them were doubtless put out by very poor parents to save funeral expenses. In hard times the number of dead and live foundlings always increases very noticeably. But whether travelling by way of the Morgue or the Infants' Hospital, the little army of waifs meets, reunited soon, in the trench in the Potter's Field where, if no medical student is in need of a subject, they are laid in squads of a dozen."

From "How the Other Half Lives," by Jacob A. Riis, 1890.

119. "Safe from the Cops," circa 1890.

120. Children of the streets, circa 1900.

121. Two little girls on a lower East Side street, circa 1900.

122. Street Arabs sleeping in a Mulberry Street areaway, circa 1890. The plight of children as a result of the overcrowding and slums was utterly tragic. Babies were abandoned to die in large numbers—cases were reported of parents speculating on insurance policies on their infants' lives. Some were even buried alive in boxes. Baby farms, for a fee and with many pious words, would take the infants and then literally starve them to death. Thus extremes of poverty succeeded in erasing the last remnants of humanity from some of its victims. Others survived despite the slums and made the best of whatever New York had to offer.

123. The Potter's Field on Hart Island, circa 1889. Potter's Field was the name given to the successive free burial grounds for the poor which have been situated in various parts of the city during its history. At the time of this photograph one in every ten New Yorkers was destined to take his or her place among the ranks in these large open mass graves. The high incidence of infant mortality is in evidence here in the five tiny pine coffins, one of which is being lifted by the grave digger in the background.

124

Crime

As poverty bred the slums, so the slums bred crime—beyond the tenements and sweatshops the treacherous path of the poor immigrant continued even further downward. In the hovels and squalor of Mulberry Bend and the Five Points, just to the west of the Bowery by Chatham Square, lay a maze of alleys and courtyards that housed a motley crowd of ragpickers, beggars, thugs, and cutthroats. The streets were prowled continually by warring gangs sporting such titles as "the Dead Rabbits," the "Whyos," and the "Plug Uglies." Under the piers, the river pirates and gang members had their "clubhouses." Farther north in "Satan's Circus," Sixth Avenue between Twenty-fourth and Fortieth Streets was lined with hundreds of brothels, saloons, and all night dance halls, all of which paid regular sums to the police and politicians to operate unhindered. Perhaps the most amazing fact of all was that so many of the poor remained uncompromised under conditions which were so appalling that theft, violence, and prostitution would seem to have been inevitable.

124. Looking north up Mulberry Street from Park Street, circa 1890.

125. A side alley, circa 1895. This was the infamous Mulberry Bend, the center of crime in New York in the late nineteenth century. Although the street looks innocent enough, the back alleys and tenements housed an inexhaustible supply of degradation and corruption. The entire section on the left of this photograph was eventually demolished to create Mulberry Bend Park (now Columbus Park), principally as a result of Jacob Riis's disclosures.

126. Baxter Street Court, 22 Baxter Street, circa 1890. Apart from the street, this left-over bit of dirt is the only scrap of this gigantic country that these poor families have for their recreation, and even this has to be shared with the horses from the stable on the right.

127

127. Under the dump at West Forty-seventh Street, circa 1895. The last resort of the jobless, short of stealing, was scavenging the city's refuse dumps and trash cans. This ragpicker has carefully sorted out piles of rags, bones, and bottles, each of which he will sell for a few pennies. Despite the meager profit to be had from such an enterprise he would still have to pay for the privilege of rummaging here. In this way a considerable revenue was collected by the city each year from its dumps.

128. Baxter Street Alley, Rag Picker's Row, circa 1890. Among such squalor and filth it is amazing to note with what neatness the harvest of a day's scavenging is prepared, from the bundles of rags to the little pile of firewood collected by the children.

129. Bottle Alley in Mulberry Bend, 1901. This alley was not only the home of bottle scavengers and headquarters of the Whyo Gang but was also the scene of dozens of murders over the years. The building is what was known as a "rear tenement," built in the center of the block at the back of the original dwellings. Some areas became solid with these structures, each of which was packed with so many occupants that the normal slum tenement would have seemed luxurious by comparison.

130. Bandit's Roost, circa 1895. This, the last of the four photographs by Jacob Riis on this page, gives a vivid impression of "the Bend" in the late nineteenth century and demonstrates the forceful way he used photography to bring such conditions to the public attention. His lifelong ambition to bring about the end of such squalor was eventually successful when the entire area was razed to construct what is now Columbus Park.

128

129

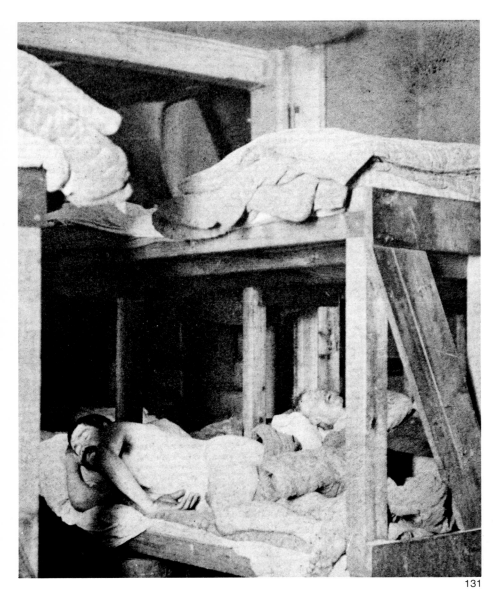

131

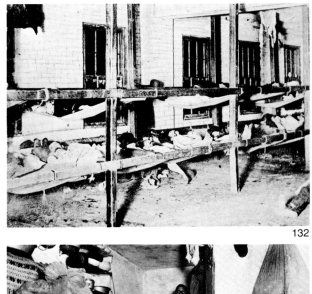

132

133

134

131. A hot summer night in a ten-cent lodginghouse, circa 1890. Bad as slums were, at least they could be considered permanent. For the newcomer to the city or the newly homeless, the Bowery provided a variety of lodginghouses whose rates were a devastating and accurate indication of the fortune of their clients. For twenty-five cents the lodger got a screen enclosing a cot and a locker, while crooks waited to recruit the innocent clerks and mechanics whose wages would not stretch to private lodgings. At fifteen cents the screen disappeared and the criminal element was well in attendance. At ten cents the locker disappeared, for now you were a tramp and no longer had need of one. For seven cents there was a long row of canvas strips over wooden supports. Finally, five cents and two cents bought a spot on the floor or table of a crowded room or all-night "restaurant."

132. Happy Jack's Canvas Palace in Pell Street, a seven-cent lodginghouse, circa 1890. On the night of this photograph the establishment was so busy that the floor was all that was available for the man whose feet are just visible on the right. Oversleeping was prevented by simply untying the hammocks.

"What place is this, to which the squalid street conducts us? A kind of square of leprous houses, some of which are attainable only by crazy wooden stairs without. What lies beyond this tottering flight of steps, that creaks beneath our tread?–a miserable room, lighted by one dim candle, and destitute of all comfort, save that which may be hidden in a wretched bed.... They have a charcoal fire within; there is a smell of singeing clothes, or flesh, so close they gather around the brazier; and vapours issue forth that blind and suffocate. From every corner, as you glance about you in these dark retreats, some figure crawls half-awakened, as if the judgment-hour were near at hand, and every obscene grave were giving up its dead."

From "American Notes," by Charles Dickens, describing his visit in 1842.

133. A crowded room in a Bayard Street tenement house, "five cents a spot," circa 1890. The accompanying quotation by Jacob A. Riis, who took all the photographs on this page, describes the visit on which this particular photograph was taken. "From midnight till far into the small hours of the morning the policeman's thundering rap on closed doors is heard, gathering evidence of illegal overcrowding. The doors are opened unwillingly enough—upon such scenes as the one presented in the picture. It was photographed by flashlight on just such a visit. In a room not thirteen feet either way slept twelve men and women, two or three in bunks set in a sort of alcove, the rest on the floor.... A baby's fretful wail came from an adjoining hall-room, where, in the semi-darkness, three recumbent figures could be made out.... Most of the men were lodgers, who slept there for five cents a spot."

134. A stale-beer dive or "two-cent restaurant" in "the Bend," circa 1885. With your can of beer, collected from brewer's dregs and doctored to put a froth on it, came the privilege of a place to sleep, usually propped up on a table or barrel, for the night. An alternative beverage known as "hot punch" consisted of whiskey, hot rum, camphor, benzine, and cocaine sweepings, and was sold for six cents a glass. Some owners of these establishments accumulated considerable fortunes even at these prices. In the winter, the sanitary police would often round up these tramps, vaccinate them, and on occasion deliver them to a recruiting office or a steamer in the hope that earning some honest wages would reform them.

135. Lodgers in the Elizabeth Street police station, circa 1890. As a last resort the police provided free lodgings on wooden boards propped up at an angle, one of which can be seen in the foreground. Police figures show that more than five million nights' lodging of this type were assigned in one year during the 1880s, indicating approximately fifteen thousand homeless.

136

136. An opium smoker in a Mott Street fan-tan den, circa 1885. In additon to the dives and bars of the Bend, adjacent Chinatown added the attraction of opium. While the Chinese seemed more able to control their own use of the drug, Westerners rapidly became addicted to its effects and dens such as this abounded both within Chinatown and elsewhere in the city.

137. The Short Tail Gang under the Pier at the foot of Jackson Street, Corlears Hook; photographed by Jacob A. Riis from a police boat, circa 1890. It is interesting to note that in the 1890s, with communications still in their infancy, these desperate criminals had no fear of being photographed. Gangs were passing their heyday by this time, but many survived until the election of Mayor John Purroy Mitchel in 1914, when more than a hundred thugs were locked up after a gang war in St. Marks Place in which labor unions were also implicated.

138. Dock rats and river thieves being pursued by the police under the piers at night, circa 1890. In his report to the mayor in 1850, the police commissioner estimated there were between four and five hundred river pirates in the Fourth Ward, the area bounded by Chatham Square, City Hall, and the East River.

139. Boys stealing apples from a cart, circa 1890. The slums and tenements were a poor influence on those growing up there. In the Five Points there were as many prowling gangs of young crooks as old, by whom they were often used as lookouts or assistants, particularly if a ship's cable needed climbing or a porthole had to be entered. Emulating their elders, they bore such names as the Little Dead Rabbits and Little Plug Uglies.

137

139

138

"The Rock Gang, the Rag Gang, the Stable Gang, and the Short Tail Gang down about the Hook have all achieved bad eminence.... By day they loaf in the corner groggeries on their beat, at night they plunder the stores along the avenues, or lie in wait at the river for unsteady feet straying their way.... The tipsy wayfarer is their chosen victim.... Should he foolishly resist or make an outcry—dead men tell no tales."

From "How the Other Half Lives," by Jacob A. Riis, 1890.

140. A Brooklyn police officer bringing home the culprits, circa 1895. In hot pursuit of the criminal came the "leatherheads"—unless they were paid to look the other way. Although crime, politics, and the police were often on the same side at various stages of the city's history, pressure to reform was overwhelming by the 1880s and an organized police system began to evolve.

141. Photographing a rogue, circa 1885.
This carefully posed shot, supposedly taken at Police Headquarters, is a sensational exaggeration; most criminals quietly conceded to the camera without any fuss. Should any opposition have been shown, the restraint would probably not have been as gentle as that proposed here.

142. The rogues' gallery at Police Headquarters, circa 1885. Photography soon became a valuable tool in the fight against crime. This collection of "mug shots" was part of one of the first attempts at organizing a centralized detective system.

143. A page from Inspector Thomas Byrnes's "Professional Criminals of America," circa 1885. Hungry Joe Lewis, bottom row center, in addition to an impressive array of other crimes, managed to fleece Oscar Wilde out of $5,000 during one of his visits to America.

140

141

142

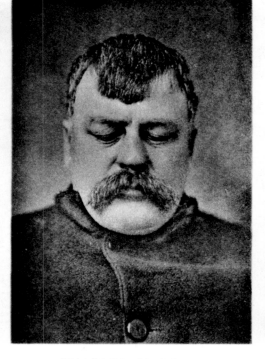

JAMES CASEY,
ALIAS BIG JIM CASEY,
BANCO AND PICKPOCKET.

CHARLES MASON,
ALIAS BOSTON CHARLEY,
PICKPOCKET AND BANCO.

PETER LAKE,
ALIAS GRAND CENTRAL PETE,
BANCO.

94

95

96

JAMES ALLEN,
ALIAS POP WHITE and DR. LONG,
HOTEL AND CONFIDENCE MAN.

JOSEPH LEWIS,
ALIAS HUNGRY JOE,
BANCO.

WILLIAM JOHNSON,
PICKPOCKET.

144. The original Tombs prison, looking south on Centre Street from Franklin Street, circa 1870. This imposing white-granite building, which contained several courtrooms and the city's cells and gallows, was the subject of much morbid curiosity and fame in its time. Although it assumed its name from the style of Egyptian funerary architecture in which it was built, it has always been shamefully symbolic of the fate of its inmates. The observations made of it by Dickens in 1842 have sadly been echoed many times since then in all of the three city jails to bear the same name. In the background can be seen the shot tower of the Colwell Lead Company at 63-65 Centre Street.

145. Handing in evidence at Police Headquarters, circa 1895. Showing a primitive form of the modern desk and rail to be found in a modern station house.

146. A detective manhandling a villain into a cell, circa 1895. Probably taken in the Tombs or at Police Headquarters. The open coal stove was the only heating for the entire cell block.

147. The "penitentiary lockstep" at Blackwell's Island Prison, circa 1900. These uniforms in the city's principal prison were intended to make the inmates conspicuous should they attempt to escape, which they sometimes did by swimming the East River. More often than not they were fished out by the police before they had got halfway.

145

146

147

"What! do you thrust your common offenders against the police discipline of the town, into such holes as these? Do men and women, against whom no crime is proved, lie here all night in perfect darkness, surrounded by the noisome vapours which encircle that flagging lamp you light us with, and breathing this filthy and offensive stench! Why, such indecent and disgusting dungeons as these cells, would bring disgrace upon the most despotic empire in the world!"

From "American Notes," by Charles Dickens, describing his visit in 1842.

148

150

151

149

Reform

Where once assistance and help, even government, was on an informal and personal basis, the rapidly expanding city of the late nineteenth century had fostered an anonymous society where the price of privacy was a tendency to overlook those in need. In response, new philanthropic institutions were born, most with religious affiliations, offering various programs of help, shelter, food, and medical care for those in trouble. Others took power into their own hands. Individual rights groups such as the women's movement made their demands heard above the din of respectable Establishment, and public opinion insisted on an end to the chaos of ineffectual city government and corrupt politics, demanding in their place adequate schools, clinics, sanitation, water supply, and police and fire services.

148. A Salvation Army Christmas kettle, looking north up Seventh Avenue from Thirtieth Street in 1906.
The Salvation Army movement, started by William Booth in England in 1865, was brought to New York by George Scott Railton in 1880. After a difficult beginning the Army soon became a powerful force on behalf of the poor, and the symbolic gesture of providing an empty cooking pot for the public to fill first appeared in the city's streets in 1898. By 1901 the donations were sufficient to finance a gigantic dinner in Madison Square Garden, a tradition continued for many years.

149. Sister Irene and some of her charges at the New York Foundling Asylum on Lexington Avenue at Sixty-eighth Street, circa 1890.
Sister Irene founded her first asylum on Twelfth Street in 1889, at which time an empty crib was left outside so that mothers, most of them unwed and from the lower East Side, could secretly deposit their unwanted infants. Despite the love and care of the sisters, it was not easy for these parentless children to survive, the mortality rate being more than 35 percent—far greater than even the cholera epidemic could achieve in the most crowded slums.

150, 151. The exterior and dining hall of the Women's Almshouse on Blackwell's Island, circa 1890.
The overcrowding here was appalling. These old women were herded together and given the bare essentials for their physical needs. They were denied any form of human affection or understanding, and indeed it is doubtful if at this stage of their pathetic lives they would have welcomed it.

152. The Kings County Men's Almshouse tailor shop, circa 1900.
This Men's Almshouse was built in 1869, and into it were crammed so many inmates that a hundred of them were forced to sleep on wooden benches. Lunch at the bare plank tables had to be made in two shifts. While the gardens provided some open space, inclement weather resulted in the day room becoming a restless mass of infirm old men, many of whom were forced to stand because of the lack of anywhere to sit.

153. Saluting the flag in the Mott Street Industrial School, circa 1895. The country's reunification following the Civil War saw a serious attempt to provide an effective educational system and was accompanied by a patriotic movement toward citizenship training. To this end many schools started the day with the Pledge of Allegiance to the flag.

154. Depositors of the Penny Provident Bank on Jefferson Street, circa 1885. In addition to the work of the school system, private projects such as this attempted to encourage independence.

155. A class being held in the Essex Street School, circa 1890. Despite the development of the city school system, overcrowding was a serious problem, as this photograph by Jacob Riis demonstrates. Notice the naked fishtail gas jets, the slate which each child holds before him, and the shaved heads of several pupils—a quick and effective cure for the lice-ridden.

156. Cooking class at Christ Church Memorial House, 344 West Thirty-sixth Street, in 1905. The increased availability of schooling, particularly to those with reasonable income, resulted in a demand for the addition of less academic subjects than mathematics and the classics. As a result, courses such as mechanics and cooking became commonplace.

153

154

155

''The question asked daily
from the teacher's desk: 'What
must I do to be healthy?' and
the whole school responds:

'I must keep my skin clean;
Wear clean clothes,
Breathe pure air,
And live in the sunlight.'

It seems little less than biting
sarcasm to hear them say it,
for to not a few of them all
these things are known only by
name.''

From ''How the Other Half
Lives,'' by Jacob A. Riis,
1890.

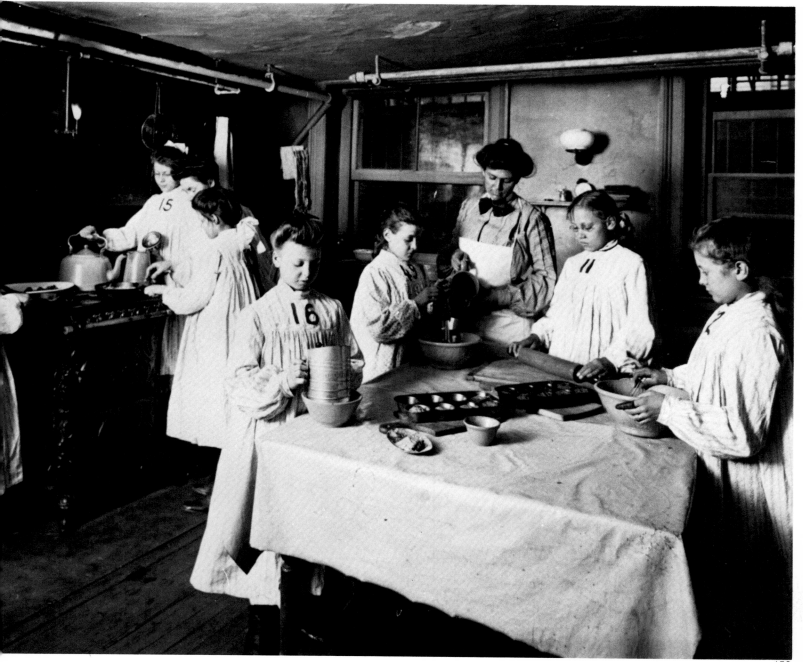

157

"She averages three dollars a week. Pays $1.50 for her room; for breakfast she has a cup of coffee; lunch she cannot afford. One meal a day is her allowance. This woman is young, she is pretty. . . . Is it anything less than a miracle if she is guilty of nothing worse than the 'early and improvident marriage' against which moralists exclaim as one of the prolific causes of the distress of the poor? Almost any door might seem to offer welcome escape from such slavery as this."

From "How the Other Half Lives," by Jacob A. Riis, 1890.

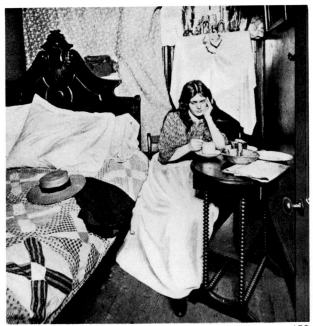

158

159

157. The Travelers Aid Society office at 28 West Fifty-fourth Street in 1909. Young women at the turn of the century were placed in a dangerous position in a society still retaining the codes and morality of an earlier time but with the growing liberation and freedom that the twentieth century made inevitable. Their innocence and gullibility, and the shame and guilt they felt for any minor transgressions, made them easy prey for white slavery and every other form of exploitation. Realizing that help at the critical moment on disembarking from the train was the key to success, the Travelers Aid Society was formed in 1907, and in these offices and the great railroad stations it directed the footsteps of the unsure toward self-reliance and security.

158. A New York working girl's home, circa 1897. Women seeking independence were confronted by very harsh conditions. While men's wages were fixed at a low but livable level, women's wages knew no such limits. At the upper end of the scale, "cash girls" earning two dollars a week had to buy their own aprons, always had to be immaculately groomed, were expected to work sixteen hours a day, and were fined for any and every shortcoming.

159. Fighting tuberculosis on the roof, circa 1900. Disease was still a major problem against which modern knowledge had made little progress, and as a consequence home cures such as this were frequently resorted to.

160. A Henry Street visiting nurse taking a short cut over the rooftops, 1908. Lillian Wald had established the Henry Street settlement on the lower East Side in 1893. It was almost a sociological certainty that the higher up you lived, the poorer you were. The visiting nurse and church missionary thus found it convenient to go from house to house via the roofs.

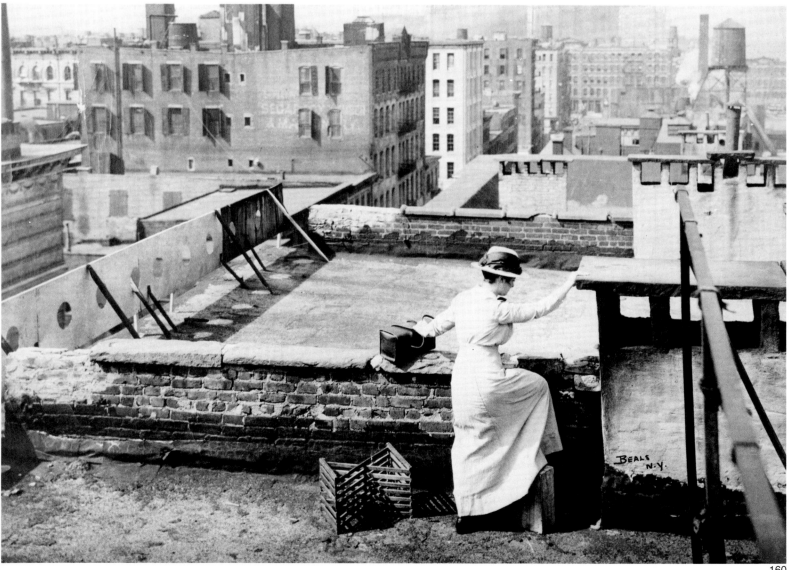

161

162

163

"Sheriff's Office of the City and County of New York, December 6th, 1875.

$10,000 REWARD

The above reward will be paid for the apprehension and delivery to the undersigned, or his proper agents, of WM. M. TWEED, who escaped from the Jailor of the City and County of New York, on Saturday, December 4th, 1875. At the time of his escape he was under indictment for Forgery and other crimes and was under arrest in civil actions in which bail had been fixed by the Court at the amount of Four Million Dollars."

165

161. William Marcy Tweed, circa 1870. By fixing elections, wholesale naturalization of immigrants (for a consideration), and sundry other "arrangements," Boss Tweed ruled the city through Mayor A. Oakey Hall for more than thirty months, during which time he managed to pocket between $50 million and $75 million for the trouble. Although his honesty was attested to by such august citizens as John Jacob Astor III, he was eventually deposed as a result of disclosures by the press, was arrested, escaped, was recaptured, and finally died in jail in 1878.

162. Tammany Hall, on the north side of Fourteenth Street between Irving Place and Third Avenue, circa 1880. Ostensibly a political club, the Tammany organization was named after a Delaware Indian chief whose statue appears in the center of the pediment. This building was infamous as the seat of Boss Tweed and the corrupt overlords of the city who controlled police, courts, and criminals alike. The small entrance on the left leads to Tony Pastor's Theatre, a famous variety house which was accommodated within the hall together with bars, restaurants, a Turkish-style conversation room, and an oyster bar. Beyond is the old Academy of Music, reminding us that Union Square was then the theatrical center of the city. The political slogans almost seem incongruous in the midst of such festivity. The one over the entrance reads "Republican treachery robbed New York of the World's Fair and delayed Rapid Transit."

163. The entrance to Tammany Hall during the 1904 mayoral campaign. George B. McClellan, son of the Civil War general, was opposing William Randolph Hearst, the owner of the *Evening Journal* which together with Joseph Pulitzer's *World* was one of the prime examples of the sensational "yellow journalism."

164. Mayor McClellan at the opening of the first section of the subway at City Hall in 1904. This magnificent study in bureaucratic elegance shows the mayor, on the right with a fur collar and his hands folded on a cane, seated next to Alexander E. Orr, president of the Rapid Transit Commission.

165. Mrs. Borrman Wells speaking at a suffrage meeting in 1907. An inevitable consequence of city life was increasing independence for women. In 1868 Susan B. Anthony's new magazine *Revolution* bore the motto "The true Republic—Men, their rights and nothing more, Women—their rights and nothing less." In the early 1870s *Woodhull and Claflin's Weekly* set Victorian America on its ear by its outspoken demand for women's rights, including freedom of sexual behavior and condemnation of the double standard. Meetings like this often created an uproar and continued to focus the public's attention on the needs of women.

166. Looking south down Fifth Avenue (left) at Forty-second Street (right), showing the Croton distributing reservoir, now the site of New York Public Library, circa 1890. The reservoir was first filled on July 4, 1842, supplying running water to the city for the first time. Its forty-four-foot-high Egyptian-style granite walls were considered one of the most inspiring sights of New York and little short of the eighth wonder of the world. When it was opened it stood well outside the built-up section of the city and thus afforded a splendid view in all directions from the promenade which encircled it atop the walls. It became a popular rendezvous for the then fashionable afternoon and evening strolls until it was demolished in 1900.

167. A policeman on duty at Fifth Avenue and Fourteenth Street in 1896. New York's original "police" were simply night watchmen carrying lanterns and wearing no uniform other than a helmet, earning them the appellation "leatherheads." The organized police force which was introduced in 1844 had a checkered career, most of it characterized by severe corruption and a pronounced lack of interest in law enforcement. Its techniques were direct, as summed up by Inspector Alexander S. Williams's famous quote: "There is more law in the end of a nightstick than in a decision of the Supreme Court." This policeman dates from a period when Tammany had been temporarily ousted as a result of the crusading clergyman Dr. Charles H. Parkhurst's disclosures and Theodore Roosevelt had been made president of the Police Board under Mayor William L. Strong's reform administration. The uniform has changed considerably over the past seventy-five years, but the contents still tend to consist of a preponderance of digestive apparatus and bulging notebooks.

166

167

168

169

168. An ash cart on Fiftieth Street in 1896.
In concert with the reform of the police under Mayor Strong, Colonel George E. Waring set about the reorganization of the Sanitation Department in 1894, resulting in the first good cleaning the city's streets had in many years and the appearance of the "White Wings," so named as a consequence of their white-duck uniforms.

169. A two-horse team racing to a fire through the streets of New York, circa 1900. Fires were a severe hazard in the old city; often they spread uncontrollably, destroying considerable areas. Volunteer fire companies, operating hand-pumped engines, and all wearing red shirts, competed violently for the honor of putting out the fire. The first mad rush was by individuals who by turning empty barrels over hydrants concealed their whereabouts until their own company's engine arrived. It was not uncommon for buildings to burn to the ground while the fire companies battled over the hydrants in the street below. In 1865 the existing force of more than four thousand belligerent volunteers was replaced by a full-time professional department.

170-172. Three views of the fire which destroyed the Equitable Building on Broadway, between Pine and Cedar Streets, January 9, 1912. Steam-powered engines such as these were first experimented with in New York in 1841 but didn't see regular service until 1857. Although feeble by modern standards, they were a considerable improvement over the old hand pumpers despite being rather temperamental—one exploded in the Bowery in 1868, killing five people. If a water source was not at hand they were often coupled to each other in a string at hose lengths, to carry water from the rivers.

Communication

It is difficult for us to imagine a society where personal conversation or a written note delivered by hand was the only means of communication. In the old city where nothing was beyond walking distance this presented no problem, but as each new row of brownstones extended its limits there came an increasing crisis of isolation. Technology responded with the telegraph, which came into widespread use during the Civil War, and then "the speaking telephone" introduced by Alexander Graham Bell to an amazed New York audience in 1878. At first regarded by the public as a toy, it was to prove one of the greatest inventions of the century, without which modern social and business life would be impossible.

173. Looking south down Broadway from the City Hall Post Office at Park Row in 1887. The change from old to new was not a comfortable one on lower Broadway. The horsecars and stages were blocking the streets in an attempt to carry the rapidly increasing population who were occupying the ever taller buildings. In the same way the sky was quickly becoming obscured by the overhead telephone wires necessary for communication.

174. Looking north up West Street from Cortlandt Street, circa 1888. This pole line, with twenty-five crossarms, had been erected in 1887 to carry wires uptown from the main exchange at Cortlandt Street.

175. Looking north up New Street past Exchange Place toward Wall Street during the great blizzard of March 11-12, 1888. With an average snowfall of three and a half feet often drifting to second-floor windows, this spectacular blizzard played havoc with the telephone system. All over the city lines collapsed under the weight of snow and ice in winds that reached 84 miles per hour, cutting off services to such an extent that connection to Boston was possible only via London, England. A law had been passed in 1884 requiring all cables to be relaid underground, but it was the fear of a repetition of this chaos which finally encouraged the work to be rapidly completed.

At first a luxury for most, the horse soon became a necessity as the most convenient source of power for all manner of work and transportation. Horses were so numerous by the turn of the century that they created a pollution problem severe even by our standards, depositing more than 2.5 million pounds of manure and 60,000 gallons of urine on the streets daily. The providential arrival of the steam engine and electricity led to a bewildering array of noisy and exotic devices for pulling the protesting public from one place to another through holes in the ground or over frail structures perched above the streets. Finally the explosive progress of the internal-combustion engine was added to the raucous din of the city just in time to welcome the arrival of the twentieth century.

176. A dead dray horse lying in a New York street, circa 1890. The lack of concern shown by these children testifies to the commonplace nature of such a sight. In the nineteenth century, horses were considered little more than an expendable commodity they were bred in farms by the thousands, shipped to the city, worked till they collapsed, and were then sold to a glue factory.

177. The Fire Department horse ambulance, circa 1900. The horses which pulled the city's fire engines were much better trained and cared for than most, and these ingenious conveyances saved many from the pistol.

178. The Horse Aid Society drinking fountain at the Manhattan Bridge entrance in 1917. The lack of any municipal action to protect horses led private organizations such as the SPCA and the Horse Aid Society to provide special stations such as these to water them properly—in this instance before the long trek over the bridge in the sweltering summer heat. In the background is the Canal Street station of the Third Avenue El on the Bowery.

179. "Free shower for horses only," 1913. Again as a protection against the lethal effects of the hot summer, this shower probably cooled down many an overworked horse and made its day less arduous.

176

177

178

179

Transportation

180

"When there is real good sleighing, my sister hires a stage sleigh and takes me and a lot of my schoolmates a sleigh ride down Broadway to the Battery and back. The sleigh is open and very long; and has long seats on each side, and straw on the floor to keep our feet warm, and the sleigh bells sound so cheerful. We see some of our friends taking their afternoon walk on the sidewalk, and I guess they wish they were in our sleigh!"

From "The Diary of a Little Girl in Old New York," written by ten-year-old Catherine Elizabeth Havens, in 1849.

181

182

183

180. A Broadway stage waiting at the Bowling Green terminal in 1872. Lurching from side to side with their rear doors swinging violently open and shut, these stages rattled and clattered up and down Broadway in their hundreds at all hours of the day and night. They were started and stopped by tugging on a leather strap attached to the leg of the driver, who, after the fare had been placed in a box beside him, made change, often inaccurately, through an aperture in the front window. Any protests from the passengers went unheeded owing to the difficulties of discussing finance with a pair of legs, all that was visible of the driver from inside.

181. A stage sleigh at Henry and Joralemon streets, Brooklyn, circa 1898.

182. Horse sleighs on Broadway near Prince Street during the great blizzard of 1888. Sleighs were an essential form of transportation in the long, cold nineteenth-century New York winters. In this view of Broadway, at the height of the telephone-wire era, two smaller vehicles are following in the wake of one of the six-horse stage sleighs which replaced the stages and horsecars when snow blanketed the streets.

183. A sleigh passing Astor House on its way north up Broadway during the great blizzard of 1888. Those who could afford to avoid the stage lines traveled in more elegant private vehicles such as these.

184. Hansom cabs in Madison Square, looking south down Fifth Avenue in 1901. Of all the horse-drawn vehicles in the city, the hansom cabs with their finely lacquered and polished finish were the most common at the turn of the century. They were named after the architect Joseph Hansom, who took out a patent for them in England in 1834, although they did not appear in New York until the 1890s. The uniformed driver, who rarely moved from his perch, could open and close the flap across the front of the passenger compartment by means of a lever at his side. This also served to imprison the occupant until the fare had been deposited in the disembodied hand which at the end of the journey would descend through a small trapdoor in the roof and, palm upward, turn inquisitively from one passenger to the other, unsure from which direction it was to be paid.

186

185. "The Terminal," by Alfred Stieglitz. A Harlem horsecar outside Astor House in 1893. These steaming horses represent man's major form of mobile power from the beginning of history until the twentieth century. Although when this photograph was taken other cities were changing over to the new electric trolleys, in New York the horse still reigned supreme and tens of thousands of them each day hauled every form of conveyance imaginable. In 1900 there were more than six thousand horses pulling these streetcars alone and it was not until 1917 that the last of these vehicles rumbled along West Street on its final journey and the days of the workhorse came to a close. The chimney led to a smoking stove, which together with a central oil lamp and a pile of muddy straw on the floor was intended to see to the passengers' every need and comfort, although by all accounts it was more successful in suffocating them.

186. The interior of a Stephenson twenty-cent "Palace Car," circa 1875. These special cars ran a luxury service for wealthy passengers on a fixed schedule. Although the structure and exterior were identical with the regular-fare cars, the furniture, carpets and decorations replaced a simple slab bench provided for poorer travellers.

187. The old Grand Central Terminal, looking west along Forty-second Street from Fourth (now Park) Avenue in 1880. The railroad was the first great practical application of the steam engine to revolutionize city life. First developed in England in the early 1800s, it soon arrived in America, where it was particularly important in reducing the vast distances of the continent to more manageable proportions. Steam locomotives first appeared on the New York & Harlem Railroad in 1839, but it was not until 1869 that the golden spike was driven at Promontory Point, Utah, and Grand Central could compete with New York's waterfront as the gateway to California. Built in 1871, this terminal had a gigantic arched iron-and-glass train shed behind its façade, reminiscent of the European stations (see plate 287). Not counting passengers from farther afield, more than 120,000 commuters from Westchester and Connecticut passed through here daily by 1900. After a face lift in 1899, the burying of the tracks below Park Avenue resulted in its demolition and the construction of the present building, which was opened in 1913.

188. The Long Island Railroad station at Manhattan Beach, Coney Island, circa 1895. This "Coney Island Exotic" station was typical of suburban stops at the turn of the century. Looking north across Sheepshead Bay, this view shows the lavish summer houses that were then dotted along the North Shore.

189. Looking east along Atlantic Avenue, Brooklyn, circa 1895. Early railroads were as much of an obstacle as an asset. Here we see the Long Island Railroad tracks when they ran down the center of Atlantic Avenue. The confusion and chaos that this situation created in rapidly developing Brooklyn resulted in their being eventually buried in a tunnel below the street.

190. A construction locomotive working on Broadway at 140th Street in 1903. The locomotive was used as a source of power on all manner of engineering projects as well as for public transportation, as demonstrated by this saddle tanker, probably one of the switching engines which used to operate on the Brooklyn Bridge (see plate 216).

187

''On it whirls headlong, dives through the woods again, emerges in the light, clatters over frail arches, rumbles upon the heavy ground, shoots beneath a wooden bridge which intercepts the light for a second like a wink, suddenly awakens all the slumbering echoes in the main street of a large town, and dashes on haphazard, pell-mell, neck-or-nothing, down the middle of the road. There— with mechanics working at their trades, and people leaning from their doors and windows, and boys flying kites and playing marbles, and men smoking, and women talking, and children crawling, and pigs burrowing, and unaccustomed horses plunging and rearing, close to the very rails—there—on, on, on— tears the mad dragon of an engine with its train of cars; scattering in all directions a shower of burning sparks from its wood fire; screeching, hissing, yelling, panting; until at last the thirsty monster stops beneath a covered way to drink, the people cluster round, and you have time to breathe again.''

From ''American Notes,'' by Charles Dickens, describing his visit in 1842.

190

188

189

194

191

192

193

191. Looking north up the Bowery from the El station at Grand Street in 1895. Every kind of ingenuity was applied to the problem of urban transportation, and the Bowery became a riot of mass transit by the end of the nineteenth century. In this view it sports two elevated tracks, the last remaining horsecar line of the four originally situated here, and the two tracks of the Third Avenue cable railroad, running from the Post Office in City Hall Park up to 130th Street in very fashionable and very white Harlem. With the exception of those still operating in San Francisco, the cable railroads in the United States were short-lived: this one, opening here in 1894, lasted only five years until it was electrified in 1899. The operator on the front platform of the southbound car, on the left, is controlling the vehicle with a large lever which gripped or released the continuously moving cable running in a circular duct below the slotted central "rail." (On the west side of the street can be seen the Gaiety Musée at 138 Bowery, where a cantor's fifteen-year-old son, later to be known as Al Jolson, first earned a few pennies.)

192. Herald Square, looking north up Sixth Avenue from the intersection with Broadway at Thirty-third Street, circa 1903. A policeman tries to bring order to a chaos of pedestrians, horses, carts, trolleys, and one of the newfangled automobiles.

193. The cable-car loop and horsecar terminal at the tip of City Hall Park, looking north up Broadway and Park Row in 1894. In front of the Post Office, two open summer cable cars and a horsecar wait to pick up passengers while more cable cars proceed up and down Broadway on the left.

194. An open-sided summer trolley at Twenty-third Street and Broadway in 1901. Owing to operating and maintenance problems the cable cars were soon converted to electrical power, the trouble-ridden moving cable being replaced by an electric rail within the central duct. The cars were unchanged in appearance, as this trolley demonstrates, seen here in the same year that the system was' converted.

195. Charles T. Harvey making the first trial trip on his "West Side and Yonkers Patent Railway" on Greenwich Street between the Battery and Dey Street in 1868. The first application of the new technology to the city's transit problem was the elevated railroad that ran along Greenwich Street from the Battery. Initially reaching only as far as Cortlandt Street, it was extended to Thirtieth Street in 1870. In many ways the nineteenth-century inventor was much more a tinkerer than a scientist, working on hit-or-miss principles. There is something magnificently incongruous about the plug-hatted, velvet-collared inventor riding his diabolical new contraption fifteen feet above a gaping crowd of disbelieving citizens.

196. Looking north along Greenwich Street in 1876. The continuously moving cable of the elevated railroad on Greenwich Street made such an appalling din that the system was abandoned and sold to the New York Elevated Railroad Company, which extended the line northward to Fifty-ninth Street and introduced steam engines, each of which bore a local or patriotic name emblazoned on its side. Although work was beginning on the other elevated railroads, this was still the pioneer system in the city.

197. The bridge entrance and Union Elevated Railroad at Sands and Washington Streets in Brooklyn, circa 1885. As the idea of the elevated railroads became accepted, ever more precarious-looking aerial structures appeared throughout Manhattan and Brooklyn.

198. Looking south down Ninth (now Columbus) Avenue from Eighty-fourth Street in 1879. Extending boldly north into the muddy wastelands of the upper West Side, New York's first El made thousands of acres of previously inaccessible land available for residential development. In the distance on the left, one of the first rows of brownstones sprouts from the barren ground.

199. The El station in Chatham Square looking north up the Bowery (left) and East Broadway (right) in 1881.

200. Looking north up Third Avenue over the elevated railroad station at Ninth Street in 1885. Between 1875 and 1880 the rapid-transit construction reached fever pitch with the completion of the Ninth Avenue extension and the new Sixth, Third, and Second Avenue lines, opening up the entire city for development by providing convenient and speedy transportation between the uptown residential and downtown business areas. The early elevated-railroad engines rained dirt and smoldering ashes on the pedestrians below, who were forced to take shelter in doorways every few minutes when one of the snorting monsters rattled overhead.

201. Looking north on Adams Street from Johnson Street, Brooklyn, in 1911. The elevated railroads changed the city physically as well as socially, creating a new kind of urban space beneath them. This characteristic New York landscape is under the approach to Brooklyn Bridge. It is regrettable that the noise and gloom eventually caused fine residential areas like this and Third Avenue in Manhattan to deteriorate badly.

202. The Sixth Avenue El station on Fourteenth Street, looking east, circa 1885. These stations, designed by Jasper Francis Cropsey, were superb examples of Victorian railway architecture, particularly in the delicacy of their ironwork and details.

199

200

201

202

203. The Warren Street station of the Alfred E. Beach Pneumatic Subway under Broadway in 1870. In this view of New York's first experimental underground railway, a car can just be seen entering from the right after its 312-foot journey alongside City Hall Park. The station surpassed even the spectacle of Charles T. Harvey's first trip on the elevated railroad (see plate 195) in its juxtaposition of the old and the new. It contained, in addition to the two statuesque light fittings in the photograph, frescoed walls, a fountain, a goldfish tank, and a pianist who above the din of the machinery attempted to soothe the waiting passengers with his renditions on a grand piano. The tightly fitting cars were propelled along the tunnel by air pressure provided by a giant steam-powered fan. Unfortunately it was more successful at sucking in the hats and packages of the pedestrians on the street above than it was at propelling the cars along the tunnel and thus the system was soon abandoned.

204. The remains of the Beach Pneumatic Subway under Broadway, circa 1910. The hole in the roof was where the air was introduced into the tunnel to propel the cars. This view shows how closely they fitted.

205. Excavation for the BMT Subway on Delancey Street in 1907. Unlike the deep tubes of London and the new Second Avenue Line, New York's subways were mostly "cut and fill," being built in a trench directly below the street, which was then replaced above them.

206. A women-only car in the Hudson-Manhattan Tube (now PATH) in 1909. The Hudson-Manhattan Tube was opened in 1908. The women-only cars were abandoned at the beginning of World War I until their revival in 1958, when the coaches were painted pink.

203

204

206

207

209

208

207. Electric cabs in front of the Metropolitan Opera House, looking east on Thirty-ninth Street toward Broadway, in 1898. The battery-powered electric motor was favored to operate the first of the commercially practical "horseless carriages"—an appropriate description of these vehicles, which were simply hansom cabs with the horse removed from the front and the motor and an extra pair of wheels added at the back. The driver with his passenger-flap lever was still occupying the same position of eminence as before (see plate 184). These cabs appeared on the city streets in 1898, but the propulsion system did not have the endurance and reliability to make them a success.

208. An electric cab in the snow, circa 1900. These later vehicles with the driver in front appeared briefly in the first years of the twentieth century. The gigantic balloon-like tires, without any treads, probably account for the driver's somewhat dejected expression as he waits for assistance while stuck in a heap of snow.

209. A damaged taxi on the Manhattan Bridge in 1918.

210. A Fifth Avenue double-decker auto stage at Forty-second Street, looking northeast, in 1910. Both cabs and buses soon made use of the internal-combustion engine. The double-deckers, which first appeared in 1908, were reminiscent of the days when passengers rode on the roofs of horse-drawn stages.

211. The Eighth National Automobile Show at Madison Square Garden, November 2-9, 1907. The first American gasoline automobile was offered for sale by the Duryea Car Company in 1896. By 1900, when the first National Automobile Show was held, more than four thousand Americans had cars. Of the thirty-one vehicles exhibited then, eight were electric, eight were steam, and fifteen were gasoline powered—a reflection of uncertainty as to the most practical propulsion system in those pioneering days. By 1907 the internal-combustion engine had triumphed, and more than 63,000 examples of the models on display here were to be built in the following year—establishing the automobile as an event in history which would radically change the social and physical structure of the country.

212. Assembling 1905 Maxwells at the Maxwell-Brisco automobile factory, Tarrytown, New York.

213. The E. W. Bonson airplane-propeller factory, circa 1910. Although sophisticated tools and machinery were being developed on all fronts, they were still firmly under the control and guidance of craftsmen. As a result, early automobiles and airplanes were still largely handmade, and remained so until after the revolution brought about by Henry Ford and his Model T in 1908. Mass production not only enabled him to sell at extremely low prices—the Model T dropped from $850 for the first model to $360 in 1917—but he was also able to offer his workmen the unprecedented sum of $5.00 a day.

211

213

There has probably never been, before or since, an event of such magnitude in the history of the city as the building of the Brooklyn Bridge. More than a simple response to the need for a safety valve to relieve the increasing pressure of population on Manhattan, it symbolized the expansion of the new culture, and its daring leap across the water demonstrated dramatically the spirit of the awakening new technology. The other bridges that followed amplified this achievement, changing the open fields of the boroughs into endless miles of brownstones almost overnight.

214. Looking east from the North (now Hudson) River across the southern tip of Manhattan toward the Brooklyn Bridge under construction, circa 1877. From the upper floor of today's office towers the bridge may seem small and insignificant, but in the 1870s its size and innovation were considered little short of a miracle. Viewed here from the other side of Manhattan, its two granite towers, each the size of a city block if laid flat, rise like cathedrals above the island, the largest stone structures on the entire continent.

215. The Brooklyn Bridge, looking southwest from Brooklyn to Manhattan in 1890. This heavily retouched photograph emphasizes those elements most prominent when the bridge was completed in 1883—the soaring towers and elegantly sweeping cables in harmony with the sleek lines of a side-wheeler in the river below. The Manhattan pier gives a vivid demonstration of its scale as compared with the skyline of the city beyond and the buildings along South Street at its foot.

216. Looking west across Brooklyn Bridge in 1885. From its very inception the bridge had included a rapid-transit system in the form of a cable railway equipped with steam switching engines which maneuvered the coaches at either end.

217. Looking west from the Brooklyn anchorage during the construction of the bridge, circa 1877.

218. Looking west toward Manhattan from the foot of Fulton Street, Brooklyn, circa 1877. This was the main crossing point between the two cities before the bridge was opened. Horsecars ran from here beside the old ferry terminal to take passengers on to all points in Brooklyn. The view of the bridge from this side must have been familiar to Washington A. Roebling, its engineer, who was crippled by the bends while working in one of the underground caissons preparing the foundation for the piers. With the help of a telescope he spent the next ten years supervising the construction from an upstairs window of his house in Columbia Heights a few blocks away.

214

215

216

The Bridges

217

218

219

220

219. Storm damage to the Williamsburg Bridge during its construction in 1898. The second bridge from Manhattan to Brooklyn was completed in 1903, not without mishap, however, when gale-force winds completely wrecked the temporary surface that bore the construction railway before completion of the final deck.

220. Looking east down York Street from Pearl Street, Brooklyn, in 1909. Everywhere the city was being invaded by engineering structures of unprecedented scale. Already the church on York Street is dwarfed by the cathedral-like newcomer at the end of the block—Pier C of the Manhattan Bridge, completed in 1909 to relieve the already overcrowded Brooklyn Bridge.

221. Looking northwest from Main Street, Brooklyn, toward the Manhattan Bridge under construction, 1909. The steel skeleton of the bridge rises from the river beyond the Catherine Street Ferry terminal, its suspension cables waiting to take the strain of the roadway being built out from the piers.

222. Looking west across Ravenswood Meadows toward Blackwell's Island (now Queensborough) Bridge under construction, 1907. The giant structure rises ominously above the rural landscape it will shortly obliterate—all this land was already earmarked as housing sites for the hordes of New Yorkers who would come pouring over the bridge when it was completed.

223. Workmen on the Blackwell's Island Bridge in 1907.

224. Looking north up the East River toward the Blackwell's Island Bridge during the placing of the final section of the lower chord in 1908. The Queensborough Bridge differed structurally from its three predecessors in being cantilevered from its supports, as demonstrated clearly by this view taken when there was still no connection between the two sides. In the suspension bridges downstream, the first step was to string across the cables, from which the rest of the structure was then hung.

225. The Mayor buying the first ticket at the opening ceremony of the Blackwell's Island Bridge in 1909. The toll rates displayed on the side of the kiosk are:

Horses without vehicles or on the lead	3¢
Single vehicles with or without one horse	5¢
Pushcarts and handcarts	5¢
Double vehicles	10¢
AUTOMOBILES	10¢

222

223

224

225

226. Looking east across Front Street below the Brooklyn Bridge in 1918.

227. Looking north up Smith Street from Bush Street, Brooklyn, alongside the Gowanus Canal, 1903.

228. The Gowanus Canal, Brooklyn, 1903.

229. The Madison Avenue Bridge, looking north from 138th Street in Manhattan over the Harlem River toward the Bronx in 1902.

So the new technology took hold and transformed the city. The shade trees which had lined the streets had given way to the barren poles supporting the harsh new incandescent lights. By day the sun filtered down through the smoke-laden and dusty atmosphere not only onto the magnificence of the great engineering feats but also onto the strange and somber industrial landscape around them. The twentieth century had arrived.

3

New New York

Although the technological revolution had hardly reached its peak, the city around the turn of the century was clearly recognizable as the complex metropolis we know today. Row upon row of brownstones were still spreading like an epidemic up the east and west sides of Central Park, and as each new bridge reached over the river, the city spread like wildfire across the countryside, consuming farms, villages, and cornfields as it went. Downtown the skyscrapers reached upward in a never-ending attempt to outclimb their neighbors. The shade trees had mostly disappeared, and there was scarcely a street whose view was not blocked by an elevated railroad or the excavation for one of the new subways.

In an effort to bring order to all this complexity a distant and dispassionate bureaucracy had developed, and in the process New York had lost much of its old personal and informal social structure. Although the local tradesmen probably still knew you by name, there was an increasing possibility that you would be visiting the big department stores on Broadway or Sixth Avenue staffed by strangers instead of neighbors and displaying goods from storerooms packed with thousands of identical items. Commerce had created millions of jobs, for women as well as men, and the increasing wages that were being earned dispensed a new liberation. The rich and the poor were still to be seen, but the middle classes symbolized the new America, flamboyantly displaying their new independence and making the streets a riot of brilliant colors and trappings that were once within the reach of only the wealthy. Home life was rapidly losing its attraction to the more glamorous entertainments of the city, and the parlor piano was being challenged by the phonograph, whose standardized metallic tones were being heard in thousands of homes across America and the rest of the world.

The following photographs, taken mainly between 1880 and 1915, show a city we can recognize despite the disguise of seventy-five years of progress. The "gay nineties" and the early years of the twentieth century were riding on the crest of spectacular social and scientific achievements in an exhilarating wonderland where nothing seemed impossible.

230. Looking southwest across the harbor and the tip of Manhattan from the east pier of the Brooklyn Bridge in 1917. Compared with the same view taken just eight years before (see plate 88), the rapid development of the city is evident. The Brooklyn Bridge and the Singer Building tower are dwarfed by the Woolworth Building, the new claimant to the title of world's tallest, and the comparatively squat Municipal Building immediately to the right of the bridge—symbolizing respectively the eminence of mass marketing and impersonal bureaucracy. In the harbor the days of sail are over; the waterfront is now a rather desolate expanse of covered piers, steamboats, and the unromantic freighters constantly pouring new wealth into the insatiable city.

Of all applications of the new technology the steamboat was one of the earliest, appearing for the first time in the early 1800s. Strangely, and in contrast to other developments, steamers took a full century to achieve final superiority on the oceans. Thus because of the persistence of such craft as schooners, photographs of the harbor and waterfront at the turn of the century often look misleadingly old.

231. The Statue of Liberty on Bedloe's (now Liberty) Island, circa 1890. Symbolizing the promise of the New World to the thousands of immigrants who each day sailed below the outstretched arm, Frédéric Bartholdi's 151-foot-high figure was a gift of the French people on the hundredth anniversary of America's independence and was finally unveiled on October 28, 1886.

232. The arm and torch of the Statue of Liberty on display in Madison Square Garden, looking north up Fifth Avenue in 1876. This mammoth amputation was exhibited first at the Centennial Exposition in Philadelphia and then in Madison Square Garden to raise money for the base and final erection. The gigantic scale of the statue is clearly evident from its comparison to the buildings beyond.

233. View across the harbor from Staten Island, circa 1900. The days of sail were not yet over, but at the turn of the century these three- and four-masted schooners would have already been considered old-fashioned by the children who were used to watching the great steamships pass by.

The Waterfront

231

232

233

234. Commuters disembarking from a Staten Island ferry, circa 1900. By the turn of the century the solitude of Battery Park had been shattered by the tramping feet of the clerks and secretaries on their way from the developing residential areas in Brooklyn and Staten Island to the new office towers along Wall Street and Broadway.

235. Looking east toward Brooklyn from the roof of the Tribune Building on Park Row, circa 1890. The new bridge arches over the East River to rapidly expanding Brooklyn. The octagonal structure on the right is one of the city's several shot towers—structures in which molten lead was poured in a thin stream from the top, breaking up into droplets which then cooled into pellets on the way down to the bottom, where they were simply shoveled into sacks.

236. Looking north up South Street toward the Brooklyn Bridge, circa 1885. In the foreground, the Fulton Ferry continued operation for several years after completion of the bridge in 1883, but as more bridges appeared and the rapid-transit systems were extended, its importance declined and it eventually closed in 1924, after 110 years of service. Beyond, connected to it, is the Fulton Fish Market.

234

235

236

237. Coenties Slip, looking east toward South Street from Pearl Street, circa 1880. The graceful curve of the new elevated railroad runs through the slip before it was filled to create Jeannette Park (see plate 248). A huddle of barges can be seen in the slip just within the top curve of the "S" where, in its original form, it still cuts into South Street. Legend has it that the name is a contraction of Coen and Antye, two lovers from Dutch colonial days who made this their meeting place.

238, 239. Oyster barges on West Street, looking north from Charles Street, circa 1890. West Street grew in importance as deeper moorings became necessary and South Street became ever more crowded. By the 1880s it was even busier than its predecessor. The Oyster Market that was located here was of considerable importance to New Yorkers who consumed the shellfish in gigantic quantities, as can be seen from the piles of shells. Behind the line of merchants' barges are the masts and sails of the fishing boats which supplied them.

240. Looking north up West Street from Chambers Street, circa 1887. Although horses are still much in evidence as they would be well into the twentieth century, the telephone poles are a sure indication of the changing order.

237

238

239

240

''West Street is quite out of the ordinary. Every conceivable kind of vehicle–dray, expresswagon, mail-wagon, furniture-van, butcher-cart, garbage-cart, beer-skid, beam-reach–is there. Sandwiched in among them or dashing across them are cabs, carriages, hansoms, automobiles. Dozens of trolley cars run across this street to the different ferry-houses; two car tracks run the full length of it, and down these tracks, perhaps in the busiest portion of the day, will come a long train of freight-cars of the New York Central Railroad. . . . No one can hear himself talk during traffic hours, except the cabbies and the truck drivers. Even they are usually purple in the face from trying to outroar the rumble, though sometimes they get blue and green with wrath when a collision takes place, and they exchange compliments about each other's driving.''

From ''The New New York,'' by John C. Van Dyke, 1909.

243

241. The side-wheeler "Providence" of the Fall River Line at Pier 28 on West Street in 1883.

242. Saloon of the "Bristol" looking aft, 1867. These squat vessels contained a gigantic central open-galleried saloon finished and decorated with exquisite workmanship. The great curving staircase led to the lower deck and the two "waisted" indentations along the sides and the central structure beyond accommodated the twin smokestacks and part of the engine room.

243. The Anchor Line's "City of Rome" docked on West Street, circa 1885. This three-funneled combination sail and steamship provides a nautical counterpart of the metamorphosis being undergone by the city. The *Savannah,* also a hybrid, had crossed the Atlantic as early as 1819, and it was not until the end of the century that sails were abandoned entirely on passenger vessels.

244. The "Lusitania" at the Cunard Line Pier on West Street arriving after her maiden voyage in 1907. Eventually sunk in 1915 by a German submarine, resulting in the loss of 1,198 lives, she looks contrastingly modern here compared to the sea of hansom cabs awaiting her passengers on West Street.

244

Commerce

The commercial capital of America had originated in the side streets along the waterfront in the days when primitive communications demanded physical proximity. The first millions had been made from the cargoes that the port attracted, but by the turn of the century it was the control of the country's financial activity which was its major source of wealth. As fortunes and power grew, new cathedrals of finance dwarfed the narrow streets and the spires of the city's churches were swallowed up as the rising skyline obliterated them.

245. Looking north from Broad Street and William Street toward the Brooklyn Bridge in 1885. For the most part the area closest to the waterfront was still covered by low conventional structures in 1885, but even here changes were beginning to appear. The El station behind the just completed Cotton Exchange (the tallest structure in the center) is on Pearl Street at Old Slip. Wall Street runs beyond it past the domed Merchants Exchange on the left, completed in 1842.

246. Looking north up Broad Street from below Exchange Place, circa 1905. The pedimented Subtreasury Building facing the camera on Wall Street is already dwarfed by the office towers around it. On the left, also with a classical façade, is the Stock Exchange built in 1903. Those who for lack of resources or reputation could not obtain a place on the exchange proper used the street—resulting in the brokers of the Curb Exchange (now the American Stock Exchange), which is represented here by the huge milling knot of people in the foreground. In earlier days when the street still contained structures of residential scale, every available front room was commandeered by brokers who by means of messages, hand gestures, and loud shouts signaled the progress of their trading to their associates in the windows.

247. The floor of the Stock Exchange in action, 1907. This unique photograph was taken illicitly with a camera concealed in a coat sleeve and smuggled past the exchange guards. The intention of the floor brokers in forbidding photography was no doubt to prevent the public from becoming aware of the ludicrous antics involved in the gambling of millions of dollars' worth of stocks.

248. An aerial view of the financial district from a balloon tethered to a barge off the South Ferry in 1906. Although Broadway and Wall Street are already lined with the new skyscrapers, this unique shot gives us a look at an area now entirely lost to the demolition gangs. The dark shape of Jeannette Park, created when Coenties Slip was filled in, is easily recognizable below the "S" curve of the El (see plates 2 and 237). At the left the Customs House is nearing completion on Bowling Green just to the right of Battery Park. In the middle the dark mass of the brokers of the Curb are visible in the roadway just below Exchange Place on Broad Street, which runs almost vertically up the middle of the picture.

246

249

251

252

253

250

249. Bryant High School Dictaphone and stenography class, 1906. The expansion of the commercial center created thousands of new clerical positions for which training was required, particularly in the use of new equipment such as this. If the Dictaphone, an application of the Edison phonograph, was shouted at loudly enough, it would record the human voice by cutting a spiral groove in a rotating wax cylinder and could be replayed by substituting earphones for the speaking tube. The typewriter was first introduced to offices in the 1870s; and was christened with Mark Twain's *The Adventures of Tom Sawyer*, the first typewritten manuscript ever published. At first there was considerable opposition to the machine from "correspondence clerks" whose precise copperplate handwriting earned them an elevated position on the office floor. It was soon discovered, however, that a female typist (then referred to as a typewriter) could perform the same job for half the wages.

250. "Success" Magazine, 32 Waverly Place, 1902.

251. The office of H. B. Marinelli, 1907.

252. The office of George Borgfeldt & Company, Importers, 119 East Sixteenth Street, 1910. These three views show the executive suite, outer office, and main floor of three typical New York business establishments. Any form of status whatsoever was accompanied by a rolltop desk—an extremely practical piece of furniture containing the entire contents of an office which could be locked at night with as much security as a separate room.

253. The art department of "McCall's Magazine" at 236 West Thirty-seventh Street in 1912. In the artistic sphere, women began to achieve some first steps toward a greater independence than menial positions in the packing department or typing pool —although even here at *McCall's*, with the exception of the fashion editor in the foreground, they were few and were all relegated to the back of the room.

255

254-258. Maillard's confectionery store in the Fifth Avenue Hotel at Twenty-third Street and its factory at 116 West Twenty-fifth Street in 1902. Among the Victorians, candy had been elevated to an art form. These exquisite handmade delicacies in the forms of flowers, figures, and even historical tableaux were not only eaten but also frequently put on exhibition. As a gift, a box of Maillard's candy was a sure and socially acceptable way to a young girl's heart. Although all the molding, finishing, decoration, and wrapping was still done by hand, a steam engine was recruited to lend muscle to the grinding, mixing and heavier tasks—on the left can be seen running overhead the power axle to which individual machinery was connected by driving belts. This fascinating series of photographs by Byron gives a unique impression of a thriving business at the turn of the century. In the inner sanctum Mr. and Mrs. Maillard and an associate strike formidable poses and, no doubt, fear into the hearts of their minions. The furnishings are archetypal: a large portrait of Mr. M., a gigantic rolltop desk, a pedestal telephone, and a polished brass spittoon. In the other departments the pecking order is clear— men handle the money and undertake the skilled work, while the women do the packing and serve behind the counter. But even this situation represented a gigantic step forward: in earlier days there was no room whatsoever in business for women, and the neat grooming of these men and women alike is evidence of the liberation that their wages have afforded them.

256

257

258

259

260

261

259. Broadway at Ninth Street, looking north outside Wanamaker's in 1898. Originally the A. T. Stewart store, this magnificent example of cast-iron architecture was built in 1859 by the architect John W. Kellum. Beyond, Grace Church and Fleischmann's Vienna Model Bakery make these two blocks, at the bottom of what was known as "Ladies' Mile," one of New York's most fashionable haunts.

260. The Sixth Avenue El station at Fourteenth Street, looking west, circa 1895. At the top right is the sign of the R. H. Macy Store at 66 West Fourteenth Street. It was founded near here at 204 Sixth Avenue in 1858 and before it moved up to Herald Square in 1902 had expanded until it occupied the ground floor of eleven different premises.

261. Looking west on Twenty-third Street from the El station on Sixth Avenue, circa 1896. As the residential areas moved farther uptown the shopping streets followed, reaching Fourteenth Street in the 1870s and Twenty-third Street in the 1880s.

262. Looking south down Sixth Avenue from Twenty-second Street, circa 1905. The main shopping center on Sixth Avenue was focused midway between Fourteenth and Twenty-third streets, and in the late nineteenth century many imposing department stores had established themselves here on "Fashion Row." On the right is the Hugh O'Neill department store, and on the left, in the distance, the tower of the Siegel-Cooper Building.

263. Looking north up Sixth Avenue from Eighteenth Street in 1899. The El which ran along Sixth Avenue and brought most of the shoppers here to "Fashion Row" was still operated by steam locomotives at the turn of the century. On the left is the B. Altman store and beyond it, with the domed tower, the Hugh O'Neill store dating from the mid-1870s.

264. The Sixth Avenue El station at Twenty-third Street in 1903. This lovely photograph by Byron conjures up the atmosphere of one of New York's most prominent shopping areas at the turn of the century, while in the foreground a hot-chestnut vendor takes advantage of the cold weather on this snowy day.

265

265. Looking north up Fifth Avenue at Forty-sixth Street, circa 1902. The Windsor Arcade, on the right, was opened in 1902 on the site of the ill-fated Windsor Hotel, which had been destroyed by fire three years before. This fashionable shopping center was built by the philanthropist Elbridge T. Gerry to provide retail and studio space for those associated with the arts such as photographers, art dealers, and glass and china merchants. The ground-floor showroom nearest to the camera, for instance, was rented by Steinway & Sons.

266. Herald Square, looking south down Broadway from Thirty-fifth Street in 1900.

267. Looking south down Broadway from Thirty-second Street in 1906.

268. Tea tasting in 1904. These photographs, all taken in the vicinity of "Fashion Row," give a further insight into shopping at the turn of the century— clearly a much more dignified ritual than it is today.

266

268

269

269. Henry H. Tyson's Fifth Avenue Market and "Ye Olde Willow Cottage" on the east side of Fifth Avenue below Forty-third Street in 1902. As late as 1905 this reminder of the Cattle Market which had existed at Forty-fourth Street, and the willow tree which gave the old inn next door its name, were still prominent landmarks.

270. The Wallabout Market, Brooklyn, circa 1900.

271. The "Farmers" Market between West, Washington, Little West Twelfth, and Gansevoort Streets, looking south, circa 1890.

272. Looking north on South Street under the arcade of the Fulton Market, circa 1895.

273. The Queensborough Bridge Market, looking west along Fifty-ninth Street toward First Avenue, in 1914. In markets such as these throughout the city, produce was delivered by the farmer or fisherman to be sold directly to the public or tradesmen. The vaulted space below the Queensborough Bridge approach, although not designed as such, became a prosperous open-air market soon after its completion in 1909. In 1916 it was enclosed with glass to protect the stalls from inclement weather and continued in operation until well into the 1930s.

270

272

273

271

274

275

276

277

274. An orange vendor on the lower East Side, circa 1895.

275. A saw sharpener on Seventh Avenue and Thirtieth Street in 1904.

276. A knife grinder on Sixth Avenue in 1894.

277. A newspaper vendor, looking north up Broadway from Thirty-fifth Street, opposite the New York Herald Building, circa 1900.

278. An organ grinder and his wife, Seventh Avenue and Forty-eighth Street, circa 1895.

279. A hurdy-gurdy man, circa 1890.

280. A street photographer, circa 1875. Street vendors and entertainers were as common a sight in the streets of New York as in the streets of the European cities from which most of them had come. Their meager earnings were diminished even further by daily rental charges for their hurdy-gurdy or other equipment. When the street people disappeared, they took with them not only their music but also their distinctive cries by which any one of them could be clearly recognized.

278

280

279

"Hot Corn! Hot Corn!
Here's your lily white corn.
All you that's got money—
Poor me that's gone none—
Come buy my lily hot corn
And let me go home."

Old street song of the Hot
Corn girls.

New York has always been famous for its architecture, not always as the object of aesthetic pilgrimage like the cathedrals of Europe but just because there is so much of it. Many of the buildings comprising the world-famous skyline are a vivid reflection of the aspirations and times of those who created them. Like the multitude of different languages to be heard in the street, they present a cosmopolitan confusion of detail in every style under the sun.

281. Broadway at Park Row and Vesey Street, looking west, circa 1895. In the center of this panorama, to the right of St. Paul's Chapel, is the Astor House. As New York's most fashionable hotel it was famous for the social stature of its guests and its internal plumbing—considered the height of luxury and a great novelty when it was completed in 1836. The Post Office on the right was opened here at the tip of City Hall Park in 1875. It was considered an eyesore from the day of its inception and was maligned constantly until its demolition in 1939.

282. Looking north over City Hall Park from the top of the A.T.&T. Building on Broadway at Dey Street, circa 1917. The Woolworth tower, left, designed by Cass Gilbert, was the world's tallest building when completed in 1913 and remained so for nearly twenty years. Beyond the Post Office and City Hall can be seen the Municipal Building, constructed at the same time. The Brooklyn Bridge terminal spanning Park Row had been entirely enclosed by this time.

283. Looking north toward City Hall Park from Nassau Street, circa 1886. Facing down Nassau Street is the old Hall of Records, whose cornerstone was laid in 1802. To the right, the *Staatszeitung* Building emphasizes the influence of the considerable German-speaking population at this time and reminds us of the days when this area was called Printing-House Square. The proliferation of open horsecars and the jumble of haphazard telephone lines are an indication of the chaos which reigned as the city made the difficult adjustments to the new mechanization.

Landmarks

284. The interior of the Brooklyn Bridge Terminal in 1905.

285. Commuters leaving the Brooklyn Bridge Terminal in City Hall Park in December 1914.
Thousands of commuters arrived from Brooklyn to start work downtown each day. Inside the glazed terminal building the crossover rails in the foreground enabled switching from one track to the other to be done electrically, replacing the steam locomotives (see plate 216) of earlier years, although the main journey across the bridge was still powered by the old cable system until 1908. Electric trains continued the service until it was entirely abandoned and the terminal demolished in 1944.

281

282

284

285

" 'I used to watch almost every rivet,' Marty said then, 'as they drove them into these skyscrapers around City Hall Park, and the higher the skyscrapers went the prouder I was of Manhattan'—and he indicated with a gaunt hand Newspaper Row where, when Marty first rode pigs in the park, stood the old Brick Church with its sloping banks of turf and the tiny graveyard."

From an interview with Marty Keese in the New York "Sun."

286

286. Looking east along Forty-second Street at Madison Avenue, circa 1885.

287. The interior of the Grand Central train shed in 1875. Built in 1871, the shed's 200-foot-span cast- and wrought-iron arches created an even loftier space than the English examples which it emulated. After modifications in 1899 it was finally demolished to make way for the present-day terminal when the tracks were relocated underground in 1913. On the left is Dr. Stephen H. Tyng's (low) Episcopal Church of the Holy Trinity, built in 1874, and in the distance the Forty-second Street station of the Third Avenue El, which connected directly to Grand Central.

288. The concourse and westbound track level of Pennsylvania Station upon its completion in 1910. Behind a massive Roman façade this truly magnificent steel and glass hall by McKim, Mead & White provided one of the greatest of all entrances to the city. Its destruction in 1963 was a tragic and unnecessary example of the myopia by which New York is constantly being robbed of its cultural heritage.

289. Madison Square Garden, looking northeast to the intersection of Twenty-sixth Street and Madison Avenue, circa 1895. This, the second building to bear the name of this site, was the result of a competition won by McKim, Mead & White. Opened in 1890, it included in addition to the large arena (see plate 211) a theater, a restaurant, and a roof garden. Despite the controversy and moral indignation regarding the nude statue of Diana by Augustus Saint-Gaudens atop its tower, it was undoubtedly one of the city's greatest landmarks until its untimely demolition in 1925. Stanford White, who spent so much of his energies designing the building, also died in it, assassinated by Harry K. Thaw in 1906.

290. Temporary wood-and-plaster ceremonial arch commemorating the return of Admiral George Dewey in 1899, looking south down Fifth Avenue at Twenty-fourth Street. Built at a cost of $35,000 and including the work of many prominent sculptors, this arch was one of several to appear in the city over the years. On the right is the Fifth Avenue Hotel.

291. Temporary German Sängerfest Arch, looking east down Twenty-sixth Street at Madison Avenue, circa 1900. On the left is the corner of Madison Square Garden and on the right the now demolished Leonard Jerome Mansion, where Winston Churchill's mother spent much of her childhood.

292. Looking south at the intersection of Fifth Avenue and Broadway at Twenty-third Street in 1889.

293. The same view during construction of the Flatiron Building in 1901. The Fuller Building, nicknamed the Flatiron as a result of its triangular plan, was designed by D. H. Burnham & Co., the first of a new type of tower which rose as a bold shaft, beginning a total revolution of the city's physical appearance. Its visual punctuation on the south side of Madison Square is clearly evident in these two photographs. Its non-load-bearing masonry curtain walls hung from a steel frame, well demonstrated here by the open interruption of the third, fourth, and fifth stories.

292

290

291

293

294

"*Leaving other parts neglected, these churches crowd on to one another. Two or three of them are on one block. The singing and preaching in one church is heard in another. Costly and elegant, most of them are thinly attended. Looking on their rich adornments, and inquiring the price of pews, one is at a loss to conceive where people of moderate means go to church in this city.*"

From "Sunshine and Shadow in New York," by Matthew Hale Smith, 1869.

126. "ST. PATRICK'S CATHEDRAL" N.Y.

295

297

294. Looking south down Fifth Avenue from Fifty-ninth Street, circa 1895. The churches and clergy of New York were always inseparable from fashionable society and in many cases amassed personal fortunes through speculation. One after another, in the 1860s, churches disposed of their valuable downtown sites and among much unheeded criticism clamored for a site uptown on fashionable Fifth Avenue. Behind and to the left of the still pristine St. Patrick's can be seen the huge roof of the old Grand Central train shed. The great sea of brownstones on the west side of the avenue is now the site of Rockefeller Center and the new Sixth Avenue office corridor.

295. St. Patrick's Cathedral, looking south at Fifty-second Street and Fifth Avenue in 1894. James Renwick, Jr.'s, neo-French Gothic cathedral was completed in 1879. Immediately to its north is the boys' quarters of the Roman Catholic Orphan Society.

296. Herald Square, looking north up Broadway and Sixth Avenue from Thirty-fourth Street, circa 1910. The New York Herald Building was designed by McKim, Mead & White and was completed in 1893. From within the delicate Venetian arcades pedestrians could watch the presses churning out the news. Other features of the building were "Stuff and Gruff," the bronze figures which struck the hours on the bell at the apex (now standing on a pedestal in the same location), and the rows of bronze owls whose illuminated eyes winked out the passing of the hours at night.

297. Times Square, looking south down Broadway (left) and Seventh Avenue (right) in 1910. The twenty-five-story Times Tower was completed in 1905 in what was then called Longacre Square. As the social center of the city, its character was very different from the gaudy desolation of today. On the left is the New York Theatre, presenting the "Follies of 1910," and beyond it Rector's Restaurant and the Cadillac Hotel.

While at the lower end of the social scale the old-law and new-law tenements provided, however inadequately, for the needs of the poor, it was the demands of the ever-increasing middle class which brought about the construction of New York's characteristic row houses. "Brownstones" were so named after the variety of sandstone once quarried in New Jersey with which they are often faced, although the term is now applied to buildings totally devoid of even the smallest ornament in that material. Uptown the rich were still building in varying degrees of extravagance along Fifth Avenue, but it was the new Dakota Apartments facing them across the park which pointed even further to the leveling of society. Here, or in the less elegant "French flats," socialites who still wished to be in the center of things set up home in fashionable surroundings at a price they could afford.

Home Life

298. A row of typical brownstones on West Forty-sixth Street, circa 1900. .

299. Looking west along Forty-second Street toward the El station at Sixth Avenue, circa 1890. In the days when the shopping and entertainment areas were farther south, the Forty-second Street area was predominantly residential.

300. Looking east along West 133rd Street toward Fifth Avenue, circa 1880. In 1811 the publication of the "Commissioner's Plan" laid out the gridiron of streets and avenues forming, after the addition of Central Park, the present road pattern. As the city expanded northward, plots of land were sold piecemeal to speculative builders who developed the blocks of familiar row houses and brownstones. These single-family dwellings in the upper city developed with astonishing rapidity between 1880 and 1910, facilitated by the appearance of the subways, cable cars, and elevated railroads.

301. Looking east down Huntington Street from Columbia Street, Brooklyn, circa 1910. Streets such as this were typical in the suburbs at the turn of the century, with timber frame and clapboard being used rather than the more durable and expensive materials to be found downtown or in Manhattan.

298

299

300

301

302

302. Looking south down Fifth Avenue from Forty-second Street in 1880. In midtown Fifth Avenue's last days as a residential street, the rows of brownstones stretch down into the distance, broken only by the mass of the Union League at Thirty-ninth Street. The strange structure with the indescribable style on the left, facing the Croton distributing reservoir (see plate 166), was the "House of Mansions," a unique venture in city living. Although the center section was occupied by Rutgers Female College, which moved here when the building was completed in 1860, it is in reality five separate private residences rather like a block of conventional houses but all sharing the same extravagant palatial exterior, a sort of row Xanadu. It was demolished in 1883 in the commercial transformation of Fifth Avenue, during which the road surface was extended over what was once sidewalk, and the sidewalk over what was stoops and gardens, totally changing its scale and character.

303. Skating in Central Park in front of the Dakota in 1894. Behind the trio of girls is the famous Dakota apartment house between Seventy-second and Seventy-third Streets on Eighth Avenue (now Central Park West). When it was completed in 1884, it stood alone in the fields. The story goes that this is how it got its name—people said it was so far away from anything it might as well be in the Dakota Territory.

304. The Navarro Flats, Central Park South and Seventh Avenue, looking east, circa 1889. To help overcome the initial prejudice against living under a common roof, these flats, completed in 1882, were divided into several separate groups, each with a separate entrance and different Hispanic name— Madrid, Barcelona, Valencia, Cordova, etc.

303

304

305

306

"*Senator Copper of Tonopah Ditch*
Made a clean billion in minin' and sich,
Hiked fer Noo York, where his money he blew
Buildin' a palace of Fift' Avenoo.
'How,' sez the Senator, 'can I look proudest?
Build me a house that'll holler the loudest–'

Forty-eight architects came to consult,
Drawin' up plans for a splendid result;
If the old Senator wanted to pay,
They'd give 'im Art with a capital A.

     Pillars Ionic,
     Eaves Babylonic,
Doors cut in scallops, resemblin' a shell;
     Roof wuz Egyptian,
     Gables caniptian,
Whole grand effect, when completed, wuz-hell."

From a poem by Wallace Irwin.

308

305. Looking north up Fifth Avenue from Fifty-first Street in 1900. Beyond St. Patrick's, from where this view was taken, Fifth Avenue made no bones about its aspirations to class and wealth. The Vanderbilts in particular had moved here en masse. On the extreme left are the twin houses completed in 1884 by Gustav and Christian Herter for William Henry (the Commodore's son) and his two sons-in-law William D. Sloane and Elliot F. Shepard. Immediately north, across Fifty-second Street, William H.'s son William Kissam Vanderbilt had taken up residence in 1881 in a house designed by Richard Morris Hunt. In the distance, at Fifty-ninth Street, the two pinnacles of George B. Post's house for Cornelius Vanderbilt II, elder brother of William K., completed in 1894, are silhouetted against the sky on the left of the street.

306. The Cornelius Vanderbilt II house, looking south down Fifth Avenue from Fifty-ninth Street, circa 1895. The character of this section of Fifth Avenue at the turn of the century is even more evident in this view looking south at the same buildings as in the previous photograph. Facing the camera and the Plaza is the carriage entrance of the thirty-servant Vanderbilt Mansion, demolished in 1927.

307. Looking north up Fifth Avenue from Sixty-fifth Street in 1898. While the Vanderbilts had invaded Fifth Avenue below the Plaza, the rest of the fasionable set, not to be left out, mounted a mass attack on the east side of Central Park from Sixtieth to Ninetieth Streets. In a determined attempt to outdo each other, this endless panorama of pinnacles, towers, and every kind of architectural knickknack imaginable stretched without interruption for a mile and a half. In the foreground, the twin house of Mrs. John Jacob Astor and William B. Astor contained a two-ton bathtub carved out of a solid block of marble. So on up the avenue, each elaborate entranceway led to ever more bizarre diversions in this aristocratic Disneyland, paid for with the great fortunes that were being accumulated in the new industrial age.

308. Looking north up Riverside Park from Seventy-second Street, circa 1911. Fifth Avenue was not the only area to invite the attention of the wealthy. Here, facing Riverside Park and occupying the entire block between Seventy-third and Seventy-fourth Streets, is the Charles M. Schwab house, completed in 1906 by Maurice Hebert.

309

310

311

309. The reposing room in a Turkish bath in 1904.

310. Parlor scene on Staten Island, circa 1900.

311. Al Smith and Family, circa 1900.

312. An Oriental-style interior, 1904. Whether in the luxury of a Fifth Avenue Mansion or a Turkish bath, or amid the humbler pleasures of homemade entertainment around the parlor piano, these views capture some of the spirit of the "Golden Nineties" and the excitement of the dawn of the new century. Perhaps the charming family group best epitomizes the aspirations of the era—a rising middle-class American family. Alfred Emanuel Smith was born in an Oliver Street tenement in 1873, just a stone's throw from the Bowery at Chatham Square. From these poverty-stricken beginnings he worked his way via the docks and fish market to becoming governor of New York State for four terms and Democratic nominee for President.

Recreation

While on the one hand inventors attempted to defeat parlor recitals by introducing the player piano and the wax-cylinder phonograph, new production and marketing techniques encouraged a more active participation by enabling Sears, Roebuck to offer a "Stradivarius Model Violin" for $1.95, a "Golden Oak Parlor Organ" for $19.90, and a "Beckwith Home Favorite Piano with Mandolin attachment" for $89. But even these delights could not compete with the new and varied diversions with which the city drew the new generation away from their homes—not as members of a family but as members of the new anonymous middle class. Evenings and weekends were no longer periods of forced inactivity but opportunities for men and woman alike to enjoy sports events, a visit to a restaurant, theater, or concert—or arrange an outing to the new and previously undreamed-of spectacle of Coney Island.

313

313. The reporters' club room at 301 Mulberry Street, circa 1900. This photograph by Jacob Riis shows the items traditional in all male sanctuaries such as this—cards, whiskey, and pinups.

314. The T. E. Fitzgerald bar, 778 Sixth Avenue at Twenty-seventh Street, in 1912. The clientele in this bar indicates the lack of any social barriers in such establishments. On the left is a typical lunch counter, no longer free as they had been in the days when competition was so fierce that generous arrays of cold cuts were displayed to entice prospective customers.

315. The interior of Steve Brodie's bar at 114 Bowery, circa 1890. Brodie, of Irish descent, was a native of the Five Points and as a boy had blacked boots and sold newspapers in City Hall Park. He was most famous for his leap from the Brooklyn Bridge into the river, as a publicity stunt on July 23, 1886, a large painting of which event was proudly displayed on the street above the entrance to his bar. The details of the interior, which was liberally lined with framed portraits of famous pugilists, are interesting; wooden slats above a pit of sawdust to soak up the spilled beer, towels to wipe froth from the fashionable mustaches of the period—this in the days before people "discovered" germs—and, as American as apple pie, the cuspidors, for spitting was somewhat of a national pastime.

316. The Café Savarin in the old Equitable Building at 120 Broadway in 1901. The ticker tape, continuously spewing out of the little glass-domed telegraphs, kept the clientele well informed of the progress of their business exploits. It was in this room that the dreadful conflagration that destroyed the Equitable building on January 9, 1912, began (see plates 170-172).

317. Elliott's Curio Tavern, Brooklyn, circa 1900.

316

317

315

318

319

321

318. Looking south down Fifth Avenue from Twenty-sixth Street in 1895. On the right is New York's most famous restaurant, Delmonico's, on one of the many sites it occupied during its history. Beyond it, between Twenty-third and Twenty-fourth Streets, is the fashionable Fifth Avenue Hotel. At the intersection of Broadway at the left a group of low structures still occupies the triangular site soon to be graced by the Flatiron Building.

319. Looking east along Forty-fourth Street across Fifth Avenue, circa 1905. On the left is Delmonico's in its ninth and final location as it moved uptown to follow the fasionable New Yorkers who considered it their mecca. This building, designed by James Brown Lord and completed in 1897, containing a varied selection of dining rooms, supper rooms, ballrooms, and "bachelor apartments." In the distance is Grand Central Terminal while on the right, just visible on the corner of Fifth Avenue, is Henry Tyson's Fifth Avenue Market (see plate 269).

320. The horseback dinner at Sherry's Restaurant, Fifth Avenue and Forth-ninth Street, in 1903.

321. The Harrison Grey Fiske dinner in 1900. The ludicrous attempts of rich to outdo each other did not stop at two-ton bathtubs and marble palaces (see plate 307). The horseback dinner, in the tradition of a previous extravaganza when an artificial lake stocked with live swans had been constructed, was devised by C.K.G. Billings, the "American Horse King," complete with rustic backdrops and turf floor covering in Sherry's ballroom. The guests consumed a multicourse meal, served by waiters dressed as hunting grooms, astride steeds brought up in the freight elevator. In a belated attempt to prevent pollution of its aristocratic circle by the unworthy, society, in the form of Ward McAllister, had in 1892 published a definitive list of the "four hundred" persons who could genuinely be considered fashionable. The number was not as arbitrary as it might seem—it corresponded to the capacity of Mrs. Astor's ballroom.

322. The Thalia Theatre, 46 Bowery, looking south from Canal Street, circa 1880. Called the Old Bowery Theatre when it was opened in 1826, its elegant façade survived four fires during its history, when it was used for all types of theatrical performance from the classics via "living newspaper" dramatizations of current events to burlesque displays such as Lydia Thompson and her British Blondes. The interior of the Atlantic Garden next door was a single gigantic galleried German beer hall where every night the music of brass bands and clinking of steins could be heard.

323. Looking north on the Bowery, just above Houston Street, circa 1895. The Lyceum Concert Garden, featuring the Curtis & Heath Minstrel Burlesque, testifies to the Bowery's earlier fame, although Union Square and the "Rialto" had already taken the limelight away from New York's original home of entertainment.

324. Looking north up Broadway, across Forty-second Street, circa 1890. Then still residential in scale, today's entertainment area is at the northern end of what was called the "Rialto," Broadway between Madison Square and Forty-second Street, home of New York's theater at the turn of the century. Ahead and to the left is the island site on which the Times Building was eventually erected.

325. Sarah Bernhardt in her suite at the Hoffman House on Broadway between Twenty-fourth and Twenty-fifth streets in 1896. New York was constantly bubbling with controversy over this famous tragedienne's frequent "farewell" tours of America, which she encouraged by her predilection for sleeping in a quilted satin coffin, keeping lion cubs as domestic pets, and routinely disregarding conventional morality. Her stunning voice made no less an impression than her extremely slender figure (by Victorian standards). One reporter recorded: "An empty carriage drove up to the Albemarle Hotel and Mlle. Bernhardt got out."

326. The Casino Theater at Thirty-ninth Street and Broadway in 1896. Opened in 1882 opposite the Metropolitian Opera House, the Casino was famous primarily for light opera. Its stage door was the most popular rendezvous for "Johnnies" seeking to ingratiate themselves with one of the Casino Girls or a member of the famous Floradora Sextette.

327. Buffalo Bill parading in New York, circa 1895. Buffalo Bill's Wild West show was a popular and famous spectacle at such places as Madison Square Garden in the eighties and nineties. William F. Cody, as his real name was, is seen here with a mass of small boys, who are following their hero through the streets of New York.

322

323

324

325

326

327

328. Sleighing in Central Park in 1897. The multitude of carriages or sleighs to be seen in Central Park each day issued forth from the stables in the side streets behind the Fifth Avenue mansions—for equestrian activities of some form or another were synonymous with any pretensions to fashionable "society."

329. The Meadowbrook Hounds, Hempstead, Long Island, in 1899.

330. The actor John Drew in polo gear at East Hampton, Long Island, in 1902. Coaching, polo, fox hunting, and horse racing achieved enormous popularity among the wealthy—possibly, it has been suggested, because horses and dogs were the only living creatures who would wish to associate with them without ulterior motive. "The Meadowbrook set" hunted near Hempstead, Long Island, and boasted the largest and finest pack of English foxhounds in the country. Such activities, untainted by any utilitarian motives, the rich considered ideally suited for their purpose—"the unspeakable in pursuit of the uneatable," as Oscar Wilde summed it up.

331. The "Tally Ho" coach, circa 1880. Owned by Colonel De Lancey A. Kane, this English stagecoach, already a relic of an earlier era, started a whole coaching fad in the 1880s and 1890s. It ran from the Hotel Brunswick in Madison Square to Pelham Bridge, a journey of two hours.

329

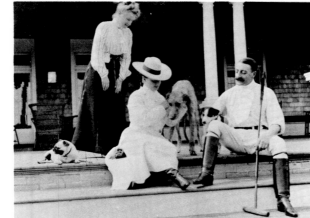
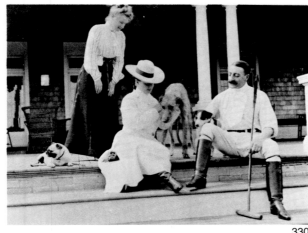

330

328

331

332

333

**332. Baseball game at the Polo Grounds, 157th
Street and Eighth Avenue, in 1906.** While something
similar to baseball existed in 1840, the Cincinnati Red
Stockings were the first professional team to be
formed, in 1869. They are seen here playing New
York on World Pennant Day. The field lies on flat
ground at the edge of the Harlem River below the
cliffs of Coogan's Bluff, which rise behind the
grandstand in this view.

**333. The League of American Wheelmen in Central
Park, circa 1885.** Between 1890 and 1896, more than
a hundred million dollars had been spent by ten
million Americans for "wheels." Despite the warnings
of certain moralists (of which there were plenty) that
"you cannot serve God and ride a bicycle," women
were also taking to the new craze, often disappearing
into parks and the countryside with their male
companions on club outings away from the prying
eyes of chaperones.

**334. The Kings County Wheelmen posing in front
of their clubhouse at 1255 Bedford Avenue,
Brooklyn, in 1889.**

334

335. Lawn tennis at Prospect Park, Brooklyn, in 1886.

336. A tennis party on Staten Island, circa 1895.

337. A tennis match on Staten Island in 1892.

338. Children's Arbor Day, Tompkins Square Park, 1904.

339. A boating party in Prospect Park, Brooklyn, circa 1885.

The new emancipation of the middle class resulted in a tremendous increase in the popularity of outings in the park, particularly to play such games as tennis, which knew no bounds of sex or social status. After its introduction to America at Staten Island it became so popular that by 1885 the Prospect Park Commission had laid out two hundred courts for use by the more than four hundred tennis clubs in Brooklyn. Alice Austen, the photographer, is standing second from the left among her friends, in the tennis group on the left.

335

338

337

339

340

341

"*Elephantine Colossus–cost over a quarter of a million dollars–Acme of Architectural triumphs–a whole seaside resort in this unique giant.*"

From an advertising card.

342

340. West Brighton Beach, from the sea, circa 1890. In the days before the boardwalk, Coney Island was well on the way to becoming the extravagant fantasy world which for years enchanted young and old New Yorkers alike. On the left is the famous wooden elephant, on the right a centrifuge, and on each side of the central open space leading up to "Niagara Falls" are hotels, dance halls, restaurants, and bathing establishments.

341. The Elephant, West Brighton Beach, Coney Island, circa 1890. Eventually destroyed by fire, this wooden elephant was a well-known curiosity in the 1890s. Entrance was effected via the large pail into which the trunk, containing a staircase, was dipped. Inside there were two main floors and an observation platform. It was variously used as a bazaar, exhibition hall, and amusement palace.

342. "The Bowery with the lid off," Coney Island. 1903. Part of Dreamland, this pedestrian thoroughfare attempted to reproduce all the thrills of the original complete with music halls, casinos, restaurants, and the inevitable German beer gardens.

343. The old Iron Pier at Coney Island in 1894. Constructed of cast iron in the best tradition of English Victorianism, this pier was eventually to become part of Dreamland. On it was constructed the largest ballroom ever made; 20,000 square feet, and from it ran four large steamers and a Santos-Dumont airship.

344, 345. Luna Park, Coney Island, in 1906. Luna Park, completed in 1903, was a spectacle of hitherto unconceived proportions. It claimed to be greater than the St. Louis's Louisiana Purchase Exposition and to have more illumination than any other spot on earth. Its forty acres included lakes swept by punts and Venetian gondolas over which a three-ringed circus was suspended. Architects, wood carvers, and florists imported from Japan built the tea garden on the right of the daytime photograph. Among the many diversions and attractions it offered were a spiral tower slide, a (simulated) trip to the moon, a German village, an old mill, a scenic railway, and a submarine journey.

346. Looking down the water chutes at Dreamland, 1906. Dreamland was Luna Park's rival at Coney Island and was completed in 1904 at a cost of more than three million dollars. It took over the old Iron Pier, re-created a "Bowery with the lid off" (see previous page), the fall of Pompeii, a haunted house, a reproduction of the Doges' Palace, a complete miniature village inhabited by 300 Lilliputians, a great firefighting spectacle, a coasting trip through Switzerland—the list goes on and on. It was adults for whom these diversions held the greatest fascination: a great fantasy world acting as an escape valve for the increasing freedom but greater physical confinement of New York as it entered the twentieth century.

"The paltry Aladdin has rubbed his lamp. Palaces have leapt aloft with gleaming minarets, lagoons are spread beneath arches of delight, the spoils of the world's revels are spilled along the beach, rendering dull and petty the stately pleasure dome that Kubla Khan decreed in Xanadu."

From "The Real New York," by Rupert Hughes, 1904.

344

346

345

347. Midland Beach, Staten Island, in 1899.

348. The Boardwalk at Asbury Park in 1898.

349. On board the S.S. "Circassia" of the Anchor Line, circa 1900.

350. Coney Island in 1877.

351. Coney Island, circa 1890. And so the dream had come true. These New Yorkers enjoying the weekend sun on the beaches around the city were not the members of some privileged class—they were shop assistants, clerks, stenographers, mechanics, and factory hands, most of them the children of the impoverished immigrants who had made the courageous decision to journey to the New World. Despite the fact that this was not the only place where such a miracle had occurred and that even here there were still whole sections of the community whose upward struggle was to take many years, these people harbored a special pride, for they came from the remarkable city whose gleaming towers rose above the harbor, the one place which more than any other had become synonymous with the glittering new twentieth century—New York.

350

348

349

351

352. Jessie Tarbox Beals and her assistant "Pumkins," circa 1900.

Photographic Credits

136 **Museum of the City of NY**
Ph. Jacob A. Riis
137 **Museum of the City of NY**
Ph. Jacob A. Riis
138 **Museum of the City of NY**
Ph. Jacob A. Riis
139 **Museum of the City of NY**
Ph. Jacob A. Riis
140 **Museum of the City of NY**
Ph. Byron
141 **Author's Collection**
Photographer Unknown
142 **Museum of the City of NY**
Ph. Jacob A. Riis
143 **Museum of the City of NY**
Photographer Unknown
144 **Museum of the City of NY**
Photographer Unknown
145 **Museum of the City of NY**
Ph. Jacob A. Riis
146 **Museum of the City of NY**
Ph. Jacob A. Riis
147 **Museum of the City of NY**
Photographer Unknown
148 **Museum of the City of NY**
Ph. Byron
149 **Museum of the City of NY**
Ph. Jacob A. Riis
150 **Museum of the City of NY**
Ph. Byron
151 **Museum of the City of NY**
Ph. Byron
152 **Museum of the City of NY**
Ph. Byron
153 **Museum of the City of NY**
Ph. Jacob A. Riis
154 **Author's Collection**
Photographer Unknown
155 **Museum of the City of NY**
Ph. Jacob A. Riis
156 **Museum of the City of NY**
Ph. Byron
157 **Museum of the City of NY**
Ph. Byron
158 **Museum of the City of NY**
Photographer Unknown
159 **Museum of the City of NY**
Ph. Jacob A. Riis
160 **Visiting Nurse Svce. NY**
Ph. Jessie Tarbox Beals
161 **Museum of the City of NY**
Ph. Mathew B. Brady
162 **NY-Historical Society**
Photographer Unknown
163 **Museum of the City of NY**
Photographer Unknown
164 **Museum of the City of NY**
Photographer Unknown
165 **Museum of the City of NY**
Ph. George Grantham Bain
166 **Museum of the City of NY**
Photographer Unknown
167 **Staten Island Hist. Soc.**
Ph. Alice Austen
168 **Staten Island Hist. Soc.**
Ph. Alice Austen
169 **Museum of the City of NY**
Ph. A. Dreyfous
170 **Museum of the City of NY**
Photographer Unknown
171 **Museum of the City of NY**
Photographer Unknown
172 **Museum of the City of NY**
Photographer Unknown
173 **Museum of the City of NY**
Photographer Unknown
174 **A.T. & T.**
Photographer Unknown
175 **Museum of the City of NY**
Photographer Unknown
176 **Library of Congress**
Photographer Unknown
177 **Museum of the City of NY**
Photographer Unknown
178 **Private Collection**
Photographer Unknown
179 **Museum of the City of NY**
Ph. Byron

180 **Museum of the City of NY**
Photographer Unknown
181 **Brooklyn Public Library**
Ph. George Brainerd
182 **Long Island Hist. Soc.**
Photographer Unknown
183 **Long Island Hist. Soc.**
Photographer Unknown
184 **Museum of the City of NY**
Ph. Byron
185 **Metropolitan Mus. of Art**
Gift of J. B. Neumann
186 **Museum of the City of NY**
Photographer Unknown
187 **Museum of the City of NY**
Ph. H. N Tiemann
188 **Long Island Hist. Soc.**
Photographer Unknown
189 **Long Island Hist. Soc.**
Photographer Unknown
190 **Museum of the City of NY**
Photographer Unknown
191 **Museum of the City of NY**
Ph. J. S. Johnston
192 **Museum of the City of NY**
Photographer Unknown
193 **Museum of the City of NY**
Ph. J. S. Johnston
194 **Museum of the City of NY**
Ph. Byron
195 **Museum of the City of NY**
Photographer Unknown
196 **Author's Collection**
Photographer Unknown
197 **Author's Collection**
Photographer Unknown
198 **Museum of the City of NY**
Photographer Unknown
199 **Museum of the City of NY**
Photographer Unknown
200 **Museum of the City of NY**
Photographer Unknown
201 **Private Collection**
Photographer Unknown
202 **NY-Historical Society**
Ph. S. A. Holmes
203 **Museum of the City of NY**
Photographer Unknown
204 **Museum of the City of NY**
Photographer Unknown
205 **Private Collection**
Photographer Unknown
206 **Culver Pictures Inc.**
Photographer Unknown
207 **Museum of the City of NY**
Ph. Van de Weyde
208 **Museum of the City of NY**
Photographer Unknown
209 **Private Collection**
Photographer Unknown
210 **Staten Island Hist. Soc.**
Ph. Alice Austen
211 **Museum of the City of NY**
Ph. Byron
212 **Museum of the City of NY**
Ph. Byron
213 **Museum of the City of NY**
Ph. Byron
214 **Long Island Hist. Soc.**
Photographer Unknown
215 **Author's Collection**
Ph. Braun, Clément & Cie
216 **Brooklyn Public Library**
Ph. George Brainerd
217 **Museum of the City of NY**
Photographer Unknown
218 **Museum of the City of NY**
Photographer Unknown
219 **Private Collection**
Photographer Unknown
220 **Private Collection**
Photographer Unknown
221 **Private Collection**
Photographer Unknown
222 **Private Collection**
Photographer Unknown
223 **Private Collection**
Photographer Unknown

224 **Private Collection**
Photographer Unknown
225 **Private Collection**
Photographer Unknown
226 **Private Collection**
Photographer Unknown
227 **Private Collection**
Photographer Unknown
228 **Private Collection**
Photographer Unknown
229 **Private Collection**
Photographer Unknown
230 **Museum of the City of NY**
Photographer Unknown
231 **NY-Historical Society**
Ph. E. Bierstadt
232 **NY-Historical Society**
Photographer Unknown
233 **Museum of the City of NY**
Photographer Unknown
234 **Museum of the City of NY**
Ph. Byron
235 **Museum of the City of NY**
Photographer Unknown
236 **Museum of the City of NY**
Ph. George Schulz
237 **NY-Historical Society**
Photographer Unknown
238 **Museum of the City of NY**
Ph. Stoddard
239 **Museum of the City of NY**
Photographer Unknown
240 **Museum of the City of NY**
Photographer Unknown
241 **Museum of the City of NY**
Photographer Unknown
242 **Museum of the City of NY**
Photographer Unknown
243 **Museum of the City of NY**
Ph. Adolph Wittemann
244 **Museum of the City of NY**
Photographer Unknown
245 **Museum of the City of NY**
Photographer Unknown
246 **Museum of the City of NY**
Photographer Unknown
247 **Library of Congress**
Photographer Unknown
248 **Museum of the City of NY**
Photographer Unknown
249 **Museum of the City of NY**
Ph. Byron
250 **Museum of the City of NY**
Ph. Byron
251 **Museum of the City of NY**
Ph. Byron
252 **Museum of the City of NY**
Ph. Byron
253 **Museum of the City of NY**
Ph. Byron
254 **Museum of the City of NY**
Ph. Byron
255 **Museum of the City of NY**
Ph. Byron
256 **Museum of the City of NY**
Ph. Byron
257 **Museum of the City of NY**
Ph. Byron
258 **Museum of the City of NY**
Ph. Byron
259 **Museum of the City of NY**
Ph. Byron
260 **Author's Collection**
Photographer Unknown
261 **Museum of the City of NY**
Photographer Unknown
262 **Museum of the City of NY**
Ph. Byron
263 **Museum of the City of NY**
Photographer Unknown
264 **Museum of the City of NY**
Ph. Byron
265 **Museum of the City of NY**
Photographer Unknown
266 **Museum of the City of NY**
Ph. Byron
267 **Museum of the City of NY**
Ph. Byron

268 **Museum of the City of NY**
Ph. Bryon
269 **Museum of the City of NY**
Ph. H. N. Tiemann
270 **Author's Collection**
Photographer Unknown
271 **Museum of the City of NY**
Photographer Unknown
272 **Staten Island Hist. Soc.**
Ph. Alice Austen
273 **Private Collection**
Photographer Unknown
274 **Staten Island Hist. Soc.**
Ph. Alice Austen
275 **Museum of the City of NY**
Ph. Byron
276 **Staten Island Hist. Soc.**
Ph. Alice Austen
277 **Museum of the City of NY**
Ph. Byron
278 **Staten Island Hist. Soc.**
Ph. Alice Austen
279 **Museum of the City of NY**
Ph. H. A. Wisewood
280 **Museum of the City of NY**
Photographer Unknown
281 **NY-Historical Society**
Ph. George P. Hall
282 **A.T. & T.**
Ph. Morris Rosenfeld
283 **Museum of the City of NY**
Photographer Unknown
284 **Private Collection**
Photographer Unknown
285 **Private Collection**
Photographer Unknown
286 **Museum of the City of NY**
Ph. George Schulz
287 **NY-Historical Society**
Photographer Unknown
288 **Museum of the City of NY**
Photographer Unknown
289 **Museum of the City of NY**
Photographer Unknown
290 **Museum of the City of NY**
Photographer Unknown
291 **Museum of the City of NY**
Photographer Unknown
292 **Museum of the City of NY**
Ph. H. N. Tiemann
293 **Brooklyn Public Library**
Ph. Raoul Froger
294 **Museum of the City of NY**
Photographer Unknown
295 **Museum of the City of NY**
Ph. J. S. Johnston
296 **Museum of the City of NY**
Ph. Byron
297 **Museum of the City of NY**
Photographer Unknown
298 **Museum of the City of NY**
Photographer Unknown
299 **Museum of the City of NY**
Photographer Unknown
300 **NY-Historical Society**
Photographer Unknown
301 **Brooklyn Public Library**
Photographer Unknown
302 **Museum of the City of NY**
Photographer Unknown
303 **Museum of the City of NY**
Ph. Byron
304 **NY-Historical Society**
Photographer Unknown
305 **Museum of the City of NY**
Photographer Unknown
306 **Museum of the City of NY**
Photographer Unknown
307 **Museum of the City of NY**
Ph. Byron
308 **Museum of the City of NY**
Photographer Unknown
309 **Museum of the City of NY**
Ph. Byron
310 **Staten Island Hist. Soc.**
Photographer Unknown
311 **Museum of the City of NY**
Photographer Unknown

312 **Museum of the City of NY**
Ph. Byron
313 **Museum of the City of NY**
Ph. Jacob A. Riis
314 **Museum of the City of NY**
Ph. Byron
315 **Museum of the City of NY**
Photographer Unknown
316 **Museum of the City of NY**
Ph. Byron
317 **Brooklyn Public Library**
Photographer Unknown
318 **Museum of the City of NY**
Photographer Unknown
319 **Museum of the City of NY**
Photographer Unknown
320 **Museum of the City of NY**
Ph. Byron
321 **Museum of the City of NY**
Ph. Byron
322 **Museum of the City of NY**
Photographer Unknown
323 **Author's Collection**
Photographer Unknown
324 **Museum of the City of NY**
Photographer Unknown
325 **Museum of the City of NY**
Ph. Byron
326 **Museum of the City of NY**
Ph. Byron
327 **Museum of the City of NY**
Photographer Unknown
328 **Museum of the City of NY**
Ph. Byron
329 **Museum of the City of NY**
Ph. Byron
330 **Museum of the City of NY**
Ph. Byron
331 **Museum of the City of NY**
Photographer Unknown
332 **Library of Congress**
Photographer Unknown
333 **Museum of the City of NY**
Photographer Unknown
334 **Museum of the City of NY**
Photographer Unknown
335 **Museum of the City of NY**
Photographer Unknown
336 **Staten Island Hist. Soc.**
Photographer Unknown
337 **Staten Island Hist. Soc.**
Ph. Alice Austen
338 **Museum of the City of NY**
Ph. Byron
339 **Brooklyn Public Library**
Ph. Raoul Froger
340 **Long Island Hist. Soc.**
Photographer Unknown
341 **Long Island Hist. Soc.**
Photographer Unknown
342 **Brooklyn Public Library**
Photographer Unknown
343 **Long Island Hist. Soc.**
Photographer Unknown
344 **Gottscho-Schleisner**
Ph. Samuel H. Gottscho
345 **Author's Collection**
Photographer Unknown
346 **Author's Collection**
Photographer Unknown
347 **Museum of the City of NY**
Ph. Byron
348 **Museum of the City of NY**
Ph. Byron
349 **Museum of the City of NY**
Ph. Byron
350 **Brooklyn Public Library**
Photographer Unknown
351 **Museum of the City of NY**
Photographer Unknown
352 **Museum of the City of NY**
Photographer Unknown
353 **Museum of the City of NY**
Photographer Unknown
354 **Museum of the City of NY**
Photographer Unknown
355 **Museum of the City of NY**
Photographer Unknown

Numbered Streets

8th Street
and 6th Ave., 27-28, 48
and The Bowery, 42-43
9th Street
and 3rd Ave., 200
and Broadway, 259
10th Street
and Greenwich Street, 31
13th Street
and 7th Ave., 148
14th Street, 260
and 3rd Ave., 162
and 4th Ave., 52
and 5th Ave., 167
and 6th Ave., 202, 260
16th Street, 252
18th Street
and 6th Ave., 263
21st Street
and 5th Ave., 54
and Broadway, 55
22nd Street
and 6th Ave., 262
23rd Street
and 5th Ave., 254-258, 292-293
and 6th Ave., 261, 264
and Broadway, 194, 292-3
24th Street
and 5th Ave., 290
and Broadway, 325
25th Street, 254-8
and Broadway, 325
26th Street
and 5th Ave., 318
and Madison Ave., 289, 291
and Madison Sq., 289
27th Street
and 6th Ave., 314
29th Street
and Broadway, 53
30th Street
and 7th Ave., 275
32nd Street
and Broadway, 267
33rd Street
and 6th Ave., 192
and Broadway, 192
and Herald Sq., 192
34th Street
and 6th Ave., 296
and Broadway, 296
and Herald Sq., 296

35th Street
and Broadway, 266, 277
and Herald Sq., 266
36th Street, 156
37th Street, 253
39th Street
and Broadway, 207, 326
42nd Street
and 4th Ave., 187
and 5th Ave., 166, 210, 302
and 6th Ave., 11, 299
and Broadway, 324
and Madison Ave., 286
43rd Street
and 5th Ave., 269
44th Street
and 5th Ave., 319
46th Street, 298
and 5th Ave., 265
47th Street, 127
48th Street
and 7th Ave., 278
49th Street
and 5th Ave., 320
50th Street, 168
51st Street
and 5th Ave., 305
52nd Street
and 5th Ave., 295, 305
53rd Street, 72
and 4th Ave., 64
54th Street, 157
and 5th Ave., 56
59th Street
and 1st Ave., 273
and 5th Ave., 294, 305-306
and 6th Ave., 68, 70
65th Street
and 5th Ave., 307
68th Street
and Lexington Ave., 149
71st Street
and Madison Ave., 62
72nd Street
and 8th Ave., 303
and Riverside Park, 308
73rd Street
and 8th Ave., 303
84th Street
and 8th Ave., 74
and 9th Ave., 198
91st Street
and 5th Ave., 67

94th Street
and Park Ave., 65
100th Street
and 4th Ave., 63
116th Street
and Madison Ave., 66
125th Street
and 3rd Ave., 32-35
133rd Street
and 5th Ave., 300
138th Street
and Madison Ave., 229
140th Street
and Broadway, 190
144th Street
and Amsterdam Ave., 75
157th Street
and 8th Ave., 332
208th Street
and Broadway, 76

Numbered Avenues

1st Avenue
and 59th St., 273
3rd Avenue, 32-35
and 9th St., 200
and 14th St., 162
and 125th St., 32-35
4th Avenue (now Park Avenue)
and 14th St., 52
and 42nd St., 187
and 53rd St., 64
and 100th St., 63
5th Avenue, 73
and 14th St., 167
and 21st St., 54
and 23rd St., 254-8, 292-293
and 24th St., 290
and 26th St., 318
and 42nd St., 166, 210, 302
and 43rd St., 269
and 44th St., 319
and 46th St., 265
and 49th St., 320
and 51st St., 305
and 52nd St., 295, 305
and 54th St., 56
and 59th St., 294, 305-306
and 65th St., 307
and 91st St., 67
and 133rd St., 300
and Broadway, 292-293, 318
and Madison Sq., 184, 232

6th Avenue, 276, 314
and 8th St., 27-28, 48
and 14th St., 202, 260
and 18th St., 263
and 22nd St., 262
and 23rd St., 261, 264
and 27th St., 314
and 33rd St., 192
and 34th St., 296
and 42nd St., 11, 299
and 59th St., 68, 70
and Broadway, 192, 296
and Herald Sq., 192, 296
7th Avenue
and 13th St., 148
and 30th St., 275
and 48th St., 278
and Broadway, 297
and Central Park South, 304
and Times Sq., 297
8th Avenue (see also
Central Park West)
and 72nd St., 303
and 73rd St., 303
and 84th St., 74
and 157th St., 332
8th Avenue, Brooklyn
and Flatbush Ave., 83
9th Avenue (now Columbus
Avenue)
and 84th St., 198

Named Streets

Adams Street, Brooklyn
and Johnson St., 201
Allen Street, 106
Amos Street (now West 10th St.),
and Greenwich St., 31
Atlantic Street, Brooklyn, 19
Baxter Street, 126, 128
Bayard Street, 133
Broad Street, 24, 245,
and Exchange Pl., 246, 248
and Wall St., 246
Bush Street, Brooklyn
and Smith St., 227
Canal Street
and The Bowery, 322
Cedar Street, 25
and Broadway 170-172
Centre Street, 144
and Chambers St., 46
and Franklin St., 144

Street Index

353. Manhattan from the air, looking north, circa 1915.

Chambers Street
and Centre St., 46
and Hudson St., 29
and West Broadway, 30
and West St., 240

Charles Street
and West St., 238-239

Chatham Street (now Park Row)
and Pearl St., 26

Cherry Street, 36-38, 104-105
and Pearl St., 105

Clinton Street
and Delancey St., 97, 115

Columbia Street, Brooklyn
and Huntington St., 301

Cortlandt Street
and West St., 174

Court Street, Brooklyn, 81
and Pierrepont St., 77

Cross Street
and Worth St., 44

Delancey Street, 205
and Clinton St., 97, 115
and Essex St., 96
and Suffolk St., 99

Dey Street
and Broadway, 39, 282
and Greenwich St., 195

Division Street
and Pike St., 98

Doyer Street
and Pell St., 102

Duane Street
and City Hall Pl., 46
and Hudson St., 30

Elizabeth Street, 107, 135

Essex Street, 155
and Delancey St., 96
and Hester St., 101

Fletcher Street, 17

Franklin Street
and Centre St., 144

Front Street, 226
and Coenties Slip, 2

Fulton Street, 15
and Broadway, 40

Fulton Street, Brooklyn, 218
and DeKalb Ave., 78
and Pierrepont St., 77

Gansevoort Street, 271

Grand Street
and The Bowery, 191

Great Jones Street
and Lafayette Pl., 50

Greenwich Street, 31, 196
and Amos St., 31
and Dey St., 195

Henry Street, Brooklyn
and Joralemon St., 181

Hester Street, 100
and Essex St., 101

Houston Street
and The Bowery, 323

Hudson Street, 30
and Chambers St., 29
and Duane St., 30
and Reade St., 29

Huntington Street, Brooklyn
and Columbia St., 301

Jackson Street, 137

Jefferson Street, 154

Johnson Street, Brooklyn
and Adams St., 201

Joralemon Street, Brooklyn,
57-58
and Henry St., 181

Lafayette Street
and Great Jones St., 50

Liberty Street, 25

Little Water Street
and Worth St., 44

Little West 12th Street, 271

Ludlow Street, 112, 114

Main Street, Brooklyn, 221

Mott Street, 136, 153

Mulberry Street, 103, 122,
129, 313
and Park St., 124

Nassau Street, 283
and Wall St., 25

Navy Street, Brooklyn
and Sands St., 317

New Street
and Exchange Pl., 175
and Wall St., 175

Oak Street
and Oliver St., 49

Oliver Street, 49
and Oak St., 49

Orange Street
and Worth St., 44

Park Street
and Mulberry St., 124

Pearl Street, 245
and Chatham St., 26
and Cherry St., 105
and Coenties Slip, 237

Pearl Street, Brooklyn
and York St., 220

Pell Street, 132
and Doyer St., 102

Pierrepont Street, Brooklyn
and Court St., 77
and Fulton St., 77

Pike Street
and Division St., 98

Pine Street
and Broadway, 170-172

Prince Street
and Broadway, 182

Reade Street
and Hudson St., 29

Sands Street, Brooklyn
and Navy St., 317
and Washington St., 197

Smith Street, Brooklyn
and Bush St., 227

South Street, 18, 236, 272
and Coenties Slip, 13, 22, 237

State Street, 19
and Broadway, 47

Suffolk Street
and Delancey St., 99

Vesey Street
and Broadway, 281

Wall Street, 24, 245-246, 248
and Nassau St., 25
and New St., 175

Warren Street
and Broadway, 203-204

Washington Street, 271

Washington Street, Brooklyn
and Sands St., 197

West Street, 241, 243-244, 271
and Chambers St., 240
and Charles St., 238-239
and Cortlandt St., 174

William Street, 245

Worth Street
and Cross St., 44
and Little Water St., 44
and Orange St., 44

York Street, Brooklyn
and Pearl St., 220

Named Avenues

Amsterdam Avenue
and 144th St., 75

Atlantic Avenue, Brooklyn, 189
and Johnson St., 201

Bedford Avenue, Brooklyn, 334

Columbus Avenue
and 84th St., 198

DeKalb Avenue, Brooklyn
and Fulton St., 78

Flatbush Avenue, Brooklyn
and 8th Ave., 83

Lexington Avenue
and 68th St., 149

Madison Avenue
and 26th St., 289, 291
and 42nd St., 286
and 71st St., 62
and 116th St., 66
and 138th St., 229
and Madison Sq., 289

Park Avenue
and 42nd St., 187
and 53rd St., 64
and 94th St., 65
and 100th St., 63

Miscellaneous

Battery Place
and Broadway, 23, 36

Bloomingdale Lane, 71

Bowery, 315, 322
and 8th St., 42-43
and Canal St., 322
and Chatham Sq., 41, 199
and East Broadway, 199
and Grand St., 191
and Houston St., 323

Broadway, 39, 183, 248, 316
and 9th St., 259
and 21st St., 55
and 23rd St., 194, 292-293
and 24th St., 325
and 25th St., 325
and 29th St., 53
and 32nd St., 267
and 33rd St., 192
and 34th St., 296
and 35th St., 266, 277
and 39th St., 207, 326
and 42nd St., 324
and 140th St., 190
and 208th St., 76
and 5th Ave., 292-293, 318
and 6th Ave., 192, 295

and 7th Ave., 297
and Battery Pl., 23, 36
and Cedar St., 170-172
and Columbus Circle, 354
and Dey St., 39, 281
and Fulton St., 40
and Herald Sq., 192, 266, 295
and Park Row, 38, 116, 173,
193, 281
and Pine St., 170-172
and Prince St., 182
and State St., 47
and Times Sq., 297
and Vesey St., 281
and Warren St., 203-204

Central Park South
and 7th Ave., 304

Central Park West (see also
8th Avenue)
and 72nd St., 303
and 73rd St., 303
and 84th St., 74

Chatham Square, 41, 199

City Hall Place
and Duane St., 46

Coenties Slip, 2, 13, 22, 237, 248

Columbus Circle, 354

East Broadway
and Chatham Sq., 199
and The Bowery, 199

Exchange Place
and Broad St., 246, 248
and New St., 175

Herald Square, 192, 266, 295

Irving Place
and 14th St., 162

Jamaica Road, Brooklyn, 85

Lafayette Place (now Lafayette
Street), 51
and Great Jones St., 50

Madison Square, 184, 232, 289

Maiden Lane, 16

Park Row, 37, 235
and Broadway, 38, 116, 173,
193, 281
and Pearl St., 16

Peck Slip, 14

Riverside Park
and 72nd St., 308

Times Square, 297

Waverley Place, 250

West Broadway
and Chambers St., 30

Map of lower Manhattan in 1860 showing early street pattern and names.

A.T. & T. Building, 282
Academy of Music, 162
Altman, B., store, 263
American Museum of Natural History, 62
American Stock Exchange, 246
Anderson Cottage, 53
Anthony, Susan B., 165
Ashbury Park, 348
Astor, John Jacob III, 161
Astor, Mrs. John Jacob, 307, 320-321
Astor, William B., 307
Astor House, 40, 116, 183, 185, 281
Atlantic Docks, Brooklyn, 20
Atlantic Garden, 322
Austen, Alice, 59-60, 116
Automobile Show, 211

BMT Subway, 205
Bandits' Roost, 130
Bartholdi, Frederic, 231
Baseball, 332
Battery Park, 10, 19, 91-92, 234, 248
Beach, Alfred E. (pneumatic subway), 203-204
Beals, J. H., 12
Beals, Jessie Tarbox, 117-118, 352
Bedloes Island, 231
Bernhardt, Sarah, 325
Bicycles, 333-334
Billings, C. K. G., 320
Blackwell's Island, 150-151
Blackwell's Island Bridge, 222-225, 273
Blackwell's Island Prison, 147
Bloomingdale Village, 71
Boating, 339
Bohemians, 113
Bonson, E. W., airplane propeller factory, 213
Bootblacks, 115-116
Booth, William, 148
Borgfeldt, George & Company, 252
Borough Hall, Brooklyn, 77
Borrmann Wells, Mrs., 165
Boss Tweed, 161-162
Boulevard, 354
"Bowery with the lid off," 342, 346
Bowling Green, 23, 36, 47, 180, 248
Brady, Mathew, 21
Bridesmaids' dinner, 9
Bristol, 242
Brokers of the curb, 246, 248
Bronx River, 86
Brooklyn Bridge, 5, 12, 88, 190, 214-218, 226, 230, 235-236, 245
Brooklyn Bridge Terminal, 282, 284-285
Brooklyn City Hall, 77
Brooklyn Court House, 77
Brooklyn Flint Glass Works, 19
Brooklyn Navy Yard, 21
Brownstones, 63, 198, 294, 298, 300, 302
Bruce's New York Type Foundry, 46
Bryant High School, 249
Buffalo Bill, 327
Byrnes, Thomas, Inspector, 143
Byron (photographer), 254-258, 264

Cable cars, 23, 191, 193-194, 216
Cadillac Hotel, 297
Café Savarin, 316
Carnegie Hill, 67
Casino Theatre, 326

Castle Clinton, 91-92
Castle Garden, 91-93
Catherine Street Ferry, 221
Cat Stick, 3
Central Park, 6, 62, 68-70, 303, 307, 328, 333
Central Park House, 74
Chinatown, 102, 136
Chinese Exclusion Act, 102
Christ Church Memorial House, 156
Cigarmakers, 113
Circassia, 349
City Hall, 164, 282
City Hall Park, 37-40, 193, 203, 281-283
"City of New York" (balloon), 70
City of Rome, 243
Clinton, DeWitt, 49
Clinton Wharf, Brooklyn, 20
Clipper ships, 16, 19
Coaching, 329-331
Cody, William F., 327
Coffee House Slip, 18
Collect Pond, 44
Colonade Row, 51
Columbus Park, 125, 130
Colwell Lead Company, 144
Commissioner's (gridiron) plan of 1811, 54, 300
Coney Island, 188, 340-346, 350-351, 355
Coogan's Bluff, 332
Cooper Union, 4
Cotton Exchange, 245
Croton distributing reservoir, 166, 302
Crystal Palace, 11
Curtis & Heath Minstrel Burlesque, 323
Custom House, U.S., 23, 248

Dakota, 303
Delmonico's Restaurant, 318-319
Dewey, George, Admiral, 290
Dictaphone, 249
Dock rats, 138
Double-decker bus, 210
Downeaster, 16
Dreamland, 342, 343, 346
Drew, John, 330
Dutch Reformed Church, 54
Dyckman House, 76

Edison phonograph, 249
Electric cabs, 207-208
Elevated railroad, 2, 98, 106, 178, 191, 195-202, 237, 245, 248, 260, 261, 263-264, 286, 299
Elizabeth Street police station, 135
Elliott's Curio Tavern, 317
Ellis Island, 93-94
Episcopal Church of the Holy Trinity, 286
Equitable Building, 170-172, 316
Erie Railway Company, 22
Essex Street School, 155

"Farmers" Market, 271
"Fashion Row," 262-263, 266
Fifth Avenue Hotel, 254-258, 290, 318
Fire, 27-28, 85, 169-172, 177
Fitzgerald, T. E. (bar), 314
Five Points, 44, 139
Flatiron Building, 293, 318
Fleischmann's Vienna Model Bakery, 259
Floating grain elevator, 15
Floradora Sextette, 326
Ford, Henry, 212
Fulton Ferry, 14, 218, 236
Fulton Market, 14, 236, 272

Gaiety Musée, 191
Geer, Seth, 51
Germans, 283, 322, 342, 344-345
Gerry, Elbridge T., 265
Gilbert, Cass, 23, 282
Goats, 67, 74
Gotham Court, 105
Government House, 23
Gowanus Canal, 227-228
Grace Church, 259
Grand Central Terminal, 187, 286, 319
Granite crossings, 46
Great blizzard of 1888, 7, 175, 182, 183
Greenwich Village, 27-28, 48

Hall, A. Oakey, Mayor, 161
Hall of Records, 37, 283
Hamilton, Alexander, 75
Hamilton Grange, 75
Hansom, Joseph, 184
Hansom cabs, 184, 207, 244
Harlem, 32-35, 191
Harlem Bridge, 32-35
Harlem River, 229, 332
Harper's Building, 5
Harrison Grey Fiske dinner, 321
Hart Island, 123
Harvey, Charles T., 195
Hearst, William Randolph, 163
Hempstead, Long Island, 329
Henry H. Tyson's Fifth Avenue Market, 269, 319
Henry Street settlement, 160
Hine, Lewis W., 110-111
Hoffman House, 325
Horse Aid Society, 178
Horseback dinner, 320
Horsecars, 26, 38, 40, 173, 182, 185-186, 191, 193, 218, 283
Horses, 169, 176-179, 183-185, 192
Hotel Brunswick, 331
"Hot punch," 134
"House of Mansions," 302
Housing Commission, 96
Hudson-Manhattan Tube, 206
Hudson River Railroad, 30
Hugh O'Neill department store, 262-263
"Hungry Joe Lewis," 143
Hurdy-gurdy man, 279
Hyde ball, 8

Icehouse, 83
Immigrants, 66, 83, 89, 91-93, 96, 99-101, 161
Irish, 104-105
Italians, 103-105

James W. Wadsworth, 95
Jeannette Park, 237, 248
Jefferson Market, 27-28
Jerome, Leonard, Mansion, 291
Jews, 96, 99-102
Jolson, Al, 191

Kane, De Lancey A., Colonel, 331
Kellum, John W., 259
Kennedy, Thomas W., 16
King George III, 36
Kings County Men's Almshouse, 152
Kings County Wheelmen, 334
Knife grinder, 276

LaGrange Terrace, 51
League of American Wheelmen, 333
"Leatherheads," 140, 167
Lincoln, Abraham, 4
Lind, Jenny, 91-92
"Little Dead Rabbits," 139
"Little Plug Uglies," 139

Locomotives, 30, 187-190, 199-200, 216, 263, 285
Lodginghouses, 131-133
Loew footbridge, 40
Longacre Square, 297
Long Island Rail Road, 188-189
Lord, James Brown, 319
Lowe, T. S. C., Professor, 70
Lower East Side, 96, 99-100, 106, 121, 149, 274, 279
Luna Park, 344-345
Lusitania, 244
Lyceum Concert Garden, 323

Macy, R. H. (store), 260
Madison Avenue Bridge, 299
Madison Square Garden, 148, 211, 232, 289, 291
Maillard's Confectionery Store, 254-258
Manhattan Bridge, 178, 209, 220-221
Marinelli, H. B., 251
Markets, 27-28, 100-101, 236, 238-239, 269-273
Marsh's Harlem Drugstore, 32-35
Maxwell-Briscol automobile factory, 212
McAllister, Ward, 320-321
McCall's Magazine, 253
McClellan, George B., Mayor, 163-164
McKim, Mead & White, 288-289, 296
Meadowbrook Hounds, 329
Merchants Exchange, 245
Metropolitan Opera House, 207, 326
Middle Dutch Church, 25
Midland Beach, 347
Mitchel, John Purroy, Mayor, 137
Morehead's, T. A. (store), 79
Mott Street Industrial School, 153

Mulberry Bend, 103, 124-125
Mulberry Bend Park, 124-125, 130, 134
Municipal Building, 46, 230, 282

Navarro Flats, 304
Newsboys, 115
Newspaper Vendor, 277
New York and Harlem Railroad, 32-35, 38, 63-64, 187, 191
New York Elevated Railroad Company, 196
New York Foundling Asylum, 149
New York Herald Building, 277, 296
New York Public Library, 27-28
New York Theatre, 297
New York Times Building, 37
Ninth Avenue El, 195-196, 198

Ohio, USS, 21
Old Bowery Theatre, 322
"Old Brewery," 44, 104-105
"Old Law" tenements, 96
Opium, 136
Orange vendor, 274
Organ grinder, 278
Orr, Alexander E., 164
Oysters, 14, 238-239

"Paradise Alley," 105
Parkhurst, Dr. Charles H., 167
PATH, 206
"Penitentiary Lockstep," 147
Pennland, 89
Pennsylvania Station, 288
Penny Provident Bank, Jefferson Street, 154
Philadelphia Centennial Exposition, 232
Pleasant Point Pump and Hose Company No. 1, 85
Police, 74, 133, 134, 135, 137-138, 140-142, 145-146, 162, 167, 168, 192

Police Headquarters, 141-142, 145-146
Polo, 232, 329-330, 332
Post Office (City Hall Park), 12, 39, 116, 173, 191, 193, 281-282
Post Office (Old Middle Dutch Church), 25
Potter's Field, 123
Printing-House Square, 37, 283
Professional Criminals of America, 143
Prospect Park, Brooklyn, 335, 339
Providence, 241

Quackinbush, B. and Son, 31
Queensborough Bridge, 222-225, 273
Queensborough Bridge Market, 273

Ragpickers, 127-128
Railton, George Scott, 148
Ravenswood Meadows, 222
"Rear tenements," 129
Rector's Restaurant, 297
Renwick, James, Jr., 295
Rialto, 323-324
Riis, Jacob A., 45, 103, 110-111, 125, 130, 133, 137, 155, 313
Ring, Leonard, 29
Riverside Park, 308
River thieves, 138
Rockefeller III, John D., 56
Roebling, Washington A., 218
Rogues gallery, 142
Roosevelt, Theodore, 167
Rutger's Female College, 302

St. Andrew's Church, 46
St. Joseph's Church, 48
St. Louis's Louisiana Purchase Exposition, 344-345
St. Luke's Hospital, 56
St. Patrick's Cathedral, 294-295

St. Paul's Chapel, 12, 37, 40, 281
Salvation Army, 148
Samlar, Caspar (farmhouse), 53
Sängerfest Arch, 291
Santos-Dumont airship, 343
Satterlee, George, 61
Saw sharpener, 275
Scavenger pig, 45
"School sink," 107
Schooners, 16, 233
Schwab, Charles M., 308
Seventh Regiment, 42-43
Shanties, 67-68, 73, 74, 81-82
Sheep Meadow, 69
Sheepshead Bay, 79, 188
Sheepshead Bay Church, 79
Sherry's Restaurant, 320
Short Tail Gang, 137
Shot towers, 12, 144, 235
Side-wheelers, 95, 215, 241
Siegel-Cooper department store, 262
Simcoe, 15
Singer Building, 88, 230
Sister Irene, 149
Sixth Avenue El, 202, 260-261, 263-264, 299
Skating, 68, 303
Sleighs, 181-183, 328
Slums, 96, 100-101, 104-106, 122, 129
Smith, Alfred Emanuel, 311
South Ferry, 23, 248
Staatszeitung Building, 283
Stages, 38, 40, 173, 180-183, 210
Staten Island, 233-234, 336-337, 347
Staten Island Ferry, 234
Statue of Liberty, 231-232
Steamboats, 19, 88, 90, 230, 233, 241-244
Steamship Row, 23, 36, 47

"Steerage," 90
Steinway & Sons, 64, 265
Steve Brodie's Bar, 315
Stewart, A. T., 259
Stieglitz, Alfred, 90, 185
Stock Exchange, 18, 246-247
Stony Brook, Long Island, 21
"Street Arabs," 115, 122
Street photographer, 280
Street vendors, 23, 264, 274-280
Strong, William M., Mayor, 167-168
Subtreasury Building, 24, 246
Subways, 164, 203-206
Success Magazine, 250
"Swamp Angels," 104-105
Sweatshops, 112
"Sweeney's Shambles," 104-105

"Tally Ho" coach, 331
Tammany Hall, 162-163, 167
Tanguay, Eva, 1
Taxis, 207-209
Telephone, 173-175, 182, 240, 283
Tenements, 96, 104-113, 124, 133
Tennis, 335-337
Tenth Ward, 96
Thalia Theatre, 322
Third Avenue El, 178, 191, 199-200, 286
Thompson, Lydia, and her British Blondes, 322
Times Building, 297, 324
Times Square, 297
Tombs Prison, 144, 146
Tomkins Market, 42-43
Tompkins Square Park, 338
Tontine Coffee House, 18
Tony Pastor's Theatre, 162
Travelers' Aid Society, 157
Tribune, 103

Tribune Building, 235
Trinity Church, 10, 12, 24, 39
Trolleys, 185, 192, 194
Turtle Bay, 72
Tyng, Dr. Stephen H., 286
Typewriters, 249
Twain, Mark, 249
Tweed, William Marcy, 161

"Undercrust" shanty, 73
Union Club, 54
Union Elevated Railroad, 197
Union Square, 52, 162, 323

Vanderbilt family, 305-306
Vauxhall Gardens, 51

Wald, Lillian, 160
Wallabout Bay, 21
Wallabout Market, 270
Wall Street Ferry, 18
Wanamaker store, 259
Waring, George E., Colonel, 168
Washington, George, 24, 49, 52
West Brighton Beach, 340-341
Western Union Building, 12, 39
West Side and Yonkers Patent Railway, 195
White, Stanford, 289
"White Wings," 168
"Whyo Gang," 129
Wilde, Oscar, 143, 330
Williams, Alexander S., Inspector, 167
Williamsburg Bridge, 219
Windsor Arcade, 265
Wooden elephant, Coney Island, 340-341
Woolworth Building, 230, 282
World Pennant Day, 332
Women's Almshouse, 150-151

Yellow fever, 48, 95

General Index

354. Looking north up the Boulevard (now Broadway) from Columbus Circle, circa 1895

Many people, some of them unknowingly, have contributed to the evolution of this book. I would like to acknowledge the assistance of a few of them, not in order of importance, but in the sequence with which I made their acquaintance.

Firstly, Alistair Cooke, whom I have never met but whose "Letter from America," that I heard regularly on the B.B.C., and whose infectious love for this country first fired me with enthusiasm to come and find out for myself. Also, Sir John Betjeman, whose book *Victorian and Edwardian London from old photographs* encouraged me to set off on a search for similar evidence of an old New York. There are several authors whose books about this city have been an invaluable guide, among the most notable being: John A. Kouwenhoven, author of *The Columbia Historical Portrait of New York*, Nathan Silver, author of *Lost New York*, and Grace M. Mayer, author of *Once upon a City*.

On my many visits to some of the fine collections of New York City history I received much welcomed help, particularly from Albert Baragwanath, Steve Miller, and Charlotte La Rue of the Museum of the City of New York who gave me many hours of their time and valuable assistance and whose collection, as a result, is well represented on these pages. Similarly, Mary Childs Black, Wilson G. Duprey, and Jan B. Hudgens of the New York-Historical Society made their fine collection available to me. At Brooklyn Public Library, Marie Spina was very helpful and took me on several subterranean guided tours, torch in hand, to retrieve old glass plates from decaying filing cabinets secreted away in the depths of Brooklyn.

My introduction to the publishing world was helped by Tom Rosenthal in London, who assisted me in my early steps with the project, and Susan Protter, my agent in New York, who along the way received a good percentage of some of my best bottles of vintage Port. Abner Stein, my agent in London, will have to wait until I return for his share. Buz Wyeth, my editor at Harper & Row, apart from much kind assistance, displayed a remarkable sense of dignity when he discovered my original manuscript consisted of three filing cabinets full of photographs and captions, necessitating the purchase of a new and much larger briefcase so he could take handfuls home to read on the train. I would also like to extend my thanks to all those others at Harper's with whom it has been such a pleasure to work, in particular: Joe Montebello, Dorothy Schmiderer, Kathleen Hyde, Lynne McNabb, and Lee Culpepper, who copyedited the manuscript.

I re-photographed most of the original material for this book on Kodak Panatomic X using a Nikon F with a 55 mm Micro-Nikkor on a copying stand as in many instances negatives had never before been made or were unsatisfactory. The processing and printing were undertaken by Reiter-Dulberg Laboratories Inc., where Abe Dulberg and John Chominsky, through a combination of excellent work and flattery, managed to satisfy my finicky photographic tastes.

In addition there were many, many others who gave assistance in a multitude of ways including: Gerry Boardman of the South Street Seaport, Dorothy Kearny of the Community Service Society of New York, Florence Rosenblum of the Long Island Historical Society, Raymond Fingado of the Staten Island Historical Society, Maggie Cumming, Bob Propper, and last but not least, Helga, who assisted not only with the indexing and typing, but shared in all the trials and tribulations of the creation of this book. Thank you all very much.

355. "Ah There," Coney Island, 1897.

Acknowledgments